THE JASON STORIES

The Jason Stories

by

Paul Wigmore

with

FOREWORD BY
THE BISHOP OF CHESTER

The Canterbury Press
Norwich

First published 1990 by The Canterbury Press Norwich
(a publishing imprint of Hymns Ancient & Modern Limited)
St Mary's Works, St Mary's Plain,
Norwich, Norfolk, NR3 3BH

British Library Cataloguing in Publication Data
Wigmore, Paul
The Jason stories.
I. Title
823'.914 [J]

ISBN 1–85311–009–4

*Typeset by Rowland Phototypesetting Limited
Bury St Edmunds, Suffolk
and printed in Great Britain by
St Edmundsbury Press Limited
Bury St Edmunds, Suffolk*

FOR
JOHN BARNARD

Foreword

Choirboys catch the imagination in photographs and Christmas cards and in their outward angelic looks! Now, Paul Wigmore has magnificently captured their spirit in a series of superb stories.

They will grip the youngest choir boy and girl and the oldest ex-chorister—and, indeed, everyone else who has any connection with churches.

Having read Paul Wigmore's Preface, I can well understand the way in which the attention of choirboys was riveted while the stories were being told—and the congregation were listening to the sermon. It might well be an excellent thing for choir boys and girls all over the country to hear them read aloud; certainly this book should be in their hands.

Adults, too, will enjoy the achievement of a difficult task: telling stories that have all the fun you expect from stories about boys but with a skilled and easily-handled piece of teaching in every one. Here, we are taken through the Church Year in a way that is revealing and fascinating; even though I am a Bishop I learned quite a bit from the book, as well as thoroughly enjoying it.

I give it the Choirboy Book of the Year Award! And it is for everyone.

+ Michael Baughen

Preface

I am indebted to John Barnard, the Choirmaster of a north-west London church, who decided that his twenty trebles would be better occupied during the Sunday morning sermon listening to a talk designed especially for them. He arranged for them to recess into the choir vestry and enjoy an animated twenty minutes of talks and activities.

It shortly became my turn to follow them out of the choirstalls and give one of the talks. But I had decided instead to write a short story, using it to explain something of the current season of Harvest. 'Jason and the Harvest Solo' was followed by a further thirteen and it was the enthusiastic encouragement of the audience and the kindness of The Canterbury Press Norwich that brought Jason Webb and Cedric Stevens to these pages.

By the way, Jason and Cedric: if ever you read these accounts of your adventures, do get in touch.

P.W.

Characters:

JASON WEBB

A Choirboy who sings in the choir of St Matthew's Church, in the village of Oakbridge. He tries to be efficient, upright and good at everything but is constantly prevented from being all these things by someone called . . .

CEDRIC STEVENS

The smallest and most troublesome choirboy. He has a knack of being in the wrong place at the wrong time and doing embarrassing things, often without meaning to do so. Jason gets the benefit of most disasters.

SPUD, JOHN and HENRY

Jason's closest friends and sparring partners. Spud's surname is Cater, which accounts for his nickname.

CECILIA WEBB

Jason's big sister. She is away at boarding school and has borne one of her saintly namesake's misfortunes.

OLD MAN DAVIS

The neighbouring farmer's father and Jason's adviser in all matters at which parents are absolutely useless.

Place:

OAKBRIDGE

A small village somewhere in England, five miles from the city and Cathedral of Oakchester and twenty miles from the sea at Oakhaven. St Matthew's is the Parish Church.

Contents

Jason and the Advent of Jagdish

'I tell you,' said Jason, 'he could make that barn door talk, or that bale of straw.'

'Come off it!' said Spud.

'We've heard your stories before,' said John, jumping down off the box he had been sitting on in the corner of the old derelict barn.

'I tell you Jagdish can make things talk'—Jason waved his arm round the barn—'that door, this box, the roof, Spud's left foot—anything!' The obstinate tuft of hair which stood up like a question mark—and with which he fought every morning in front of the mirror—now waved like a banner carried into battle.

The other three got up and stood in front of Jason where he sat on a pile of straw.

'All right, prove it,' said Spud.

'Yes, prove it,' said John.

'Go on,' said Henry.

'How can I?' Jason stood up. 'I can't prove it without him being here, can I! I tell you he's a venquil—a venquilotrist, or something—he can throw his voice and make it come out of anything. And if you don't believe me—'

The other three drew closer round him, boxing him in completely. 'Yes?' they said.

Jason, whose new friend from India had *not* in fact done anything more than make his dummy appear to talk, made a very rash decision. 'I'll get my Dad to ask him over to stay,' he said. His question mark of hair shook defiantly.

☆ ☆ ☆

That was Saturday. On Sunday morning at Choir Practice the Choirmaster reminded them that Advent Sunday was next week. 'Right, Decani,' he said, 'what does the word "Advent" mean?'

Spud grinned and put up his hand. 'We were watching the telly last night and there was an ad' for British Rail and the ad'vent on and on and—'

The choir groaned. 'Thank you, Spud. Now Cantoris. Yes, Jason?'

'Isn't it a sort of home for Roman Catholics?'

'No, Jason, that's a CONvent.'

'Sir,' said the smallest choirboy, 'it means "an arrival"'. Cedric Stevens smiled round at everyone. 'I know, Sir, because I had to write it out fifty times at school on Friday for locking Miss Brown in the stationery cupboard.'

☆ ☆ ☆

'Mum, Dad,' said Jason at supper the next day, 'any chance of having Jagdish over here to stay—just for a weekend, or something?'

'Oh, I should think we could manage that,' said Mrs Webb. 'Yes, you two got on well together at half-term down at Oakhaven, didn't you. Lucky he was staying at the same hotel as us.'

'It was terrific, unreal!', said Jason. 'Anyway, can he?'

Mrs Webb had also made good friends with Jagdish's mother while they had been on their weekend break by the sea, and had taken her phone number. She agreed to phone her to see what she thought about it. Then Mr Webb said, 'Didn't you tell us he was a ventriloquist? Is he any good at it?'

'Terrific! I was telling the gang about him. Matter of fact, that's why I want him to come over—to show them that he can do it—throw his voice all over the place.'

'Well, hardly "all over the place",' said Mr Webb. 'Ventriloquists can't actually make their voices come from any distance away, can they? I always thought all they can do is put their doll on their knee and make it talk without moving their lips.'

'Jagdish can, Dad, he can! I saw him! He had this Mickey Mouse dummy and he threw his voice right into it—it was just like the dummy talking!'

'Well, all I can say is that if he can actually throw his voice more than a few inches it's news to me. Still, it'll be fun watching him do it.'

'Certainly will,' said Jason, and he began twisting his tuft of hair as an awful doubt began to dawn.

☆ ☆ ☆

Homework stared Jason in the face after supper. He tried some maths but his brain wouldn't work. He tried some French but to no avail. Jagdish's voice was all he could think about. Jagdish's voice coming from the Mickey Mouse dummy on his knee. Jagdish's voice *not* coming from all over the place, as he'd told the gang. What would they do to him when they found out? At the end of homework time he had written six-and-a-half French verbs, two equations and a doodle of Mickey Mouse.

The next day, at break, he dashed into the school library and found a battered copy of an encyclopaedia. He looked up VENTRILOQUIST. Would it say that they could throw their voices across a room? His finger ran down the list of words and stopped. As he read, his hopes vanished. 'Ventriloquists,' it said, 'contrary to popular belief, cannot make their voices appear to come from any distance away further than a doll, dummy, etc on their lap.'

By breakfast the next morning he had found the solution.

'Mum, I've been thinking about Jagdish—we didn't get on all that well, and I don't think it's a good idea him coming over.'

'Oh, what a shame,' said Mrs Webb. 'I rang his mother last night and she said Jagdish would love to visit us and it's all fixed up.'

☆ ☆ ☆

'Ah, Mrs Webb, Good afternoon,' smiled the vicar of Oakbridge. 'Might I come in for a few minutes? There's something I'd like to chat about.'

Ten minutes later, with tea being sipped and biscuits munched, Mrs Webb summed up the situation. 'So,' she said, waving half a biscuit, 'what you're suggesting is that Jagdish will be invited to do his ventriloquist turn at the Missionary Concert in the church hall, but we've got to keep it a secret from everyone—even Jason and his friends?'

'Oh, yes, indubitably!' smiled the vicar. 'You see, it was Jason's friends who told me all about the marvellous things this boy Jagdish can do—throwing his voice from one side of the stage to the other, and so on. But I didn't tell them I was going to arrange for him to do it at the concert—if they knew that they'd spoil all the fun by telling all their friends beforehand. But if it's a secret, we can build up the excitement in our publicity by simply saying that a most remarkable and mysterious thing is going to be performed by a mystery visitor! And you do understand, don't you,' said the vicar, leaning forward and whispering dramatically, 'it's especially important that our little secret is kept just between us. Wonderful, wonderful!' he ended, and, in his excitement, slopped his tea.

☆ ☆ ☆

'Good afternoon, Mr Davis,' said the vicar on his way back to the vicarage. 'You won't book anything up for the 30th, will you! We have the most wonderful mystery visitor coming to the Missionary Concert—he will amaze you!'

☆ ☆ ☆

'Oh, good evening, Mrs Tripplethwaite!', said the vicar on the phone that evening. 'Now, before you tell me whatever you were about to tell me, may I give you good notice of the most remarkable thing which is going to happen at the Missionary Concert on the evening of the 30th . . .'

☆ ☆ ☆

'My Dear Sir John,' wrote the vicar in his study the next morning, 'Before I deal with the matter you have raised I should like to mention for your interest a most fascinating and almost unbelievable event which will take place at our Missionary Concert on the evening of the 30th.'

☆ ☆ ☆

By this time all Oakbridge was talking about the wonderful and mysterious event that was going to take place. There were rumours flying in all directions. Talking dogs were mentioned; a snake-charmer was forecast by the post-mistress. Jason and the gang were as mystified as the rest of the village.

'My parents actually know,' said Jason. 'But they won't tell me. Might as well talk to a brick wall.'

'Hey!' said Spud. 'Brick walls—that reminds me! When are you going to get your friend Jagdish to show us how he throws his voice into walls and things?'

'Hey, yes!' yelled the others. 'What about it, then?'

'Ah,' said Jason. He had hoped they'd forgotten all about Jagdish. 'Ah, yes. Well, he might be coming over for a weekend soon—but he's not very keen about showing off.' He ducked and ran as the others gave chase.

☆ ☆ ☆

Jagdish and Mrs Webb faced the vicar in his sitting room. The vicar looked disappointed.

'But, Jagdish,' said the vicar, 'these three boys—Spud, Henry and John—told me most definitely that you were able to make your voice appear to come from doors and boxes and cupboards—several metres away from you—they were quite positive.'

'I am very sorry, Sir, but I cannot. I just have my Mickey Mouse doll and I make him speak. I am afraid these boys were—were—'

'Having me on?' The vicar grinned in a most engaging way. Then he sat thinking. After a whole minute he looked up. 'Jagdish,' he said. 'It may interest you to know that on Saturday evening in the church hall you will most certainly make your voice come from many different parts of the stage. I shall see to it personally. And I'll explain later.'

When Jagdish and Mrs Webb had left he stood in the vicarage hallway, pondering. Then he said to himself, 'Boxes.' And after that he said, 'Someone very small.' He nodded, rubbed his hands, and went to the telephone.

☆ ☆ ☆

The church hall was packed. The lights went down, the curtains parted, and the vicar stepped into the spotlight.

'Dear friends,' he began. 'We are in the season of Advent, when we recall the time when Jesus was about to be born, but also when John the Baptist went throughout the countryside proclaiming the good news that Jesus, Son of God, who had been born in Bethlehem some thirty years earlier, was about to come to the people and show that he, the Christ, was their Messiah and would save his people from their sins.

'I've been going round Oakbridge for the past week telling you all about the coming of a mysterious visitor who would do wonderful things, and partly as a result of that you have all gathered here this evening, and it occurred to me that, by chance, this was a very good illustration of what was happening two thousand years ago when John the Baptist prepared the people for the coming, the advent, of Jesus Christ.'

Jason, Spud, Henry and John sat listening in the front row. 'And now that I've preached my little sermon,' the vicar ended, 'we must begin our show.'

The concert began. Mrs Tribblethwaite sang three solos, Mr Jackson read some poetry, the piano was severely hammered by the church caretaker who fancied himself as a jazz pianist, and then the curtain parted to reveal a dark stage.

'Bet it's a magician!' hissed Henry.

A spotlight came on and revealed a boy sitting there, cross-legged, with a large Mickey Mouse on his lap.

'Leviticus! It's Jagdish!' said Jason. He stared at the Indian boy in his unfamiliar turban and loincloth. The rotter! Why hadn't he said anything? Why hadn't anyone said anything? He began to work out how he could escape from the ragging of his friends. Because, sure enough, Jagdish had only his Mickey Mouse doll on stage.

The act went down well. Jagdish's lips never moved while he made the doll talk and the audience laughed and clapped at the swift patter. Jason began to think his friends might forgive him, they were laughing so much. Then the curtain behind Jagdish parted to reveal a green cloth backdrop, and, tight against it right across the stage, was a row of large wooden boxes. Jagdish looked silently at the audience, and a deathly hush fell. Then, from the box on the extreme left came a clear, high voice: 'I am in this box.'

'LE—VIT—I—CUS!' thought Jason. 'He *can* do it!'

From the box at the right hand end came: 'Now I am in this box.' Jason jumped up and down in his seat and Henry, John and Spud sat on the edge of theirs, eyes goggling.

From all the other boxes in turn the same voice came, while Jagdish sat cross-legged looking straight at the audience, his lips never moving. As the last box spoke, he got up and bowed deeply, and the audience roared and clapped with delight.

'Told you so, told you so!' shouted Jason, getting up and punching his friends with delight. Just then there was a

Jagdish looked silently at the audience and a deathly hush fell . . .

crash on stage and a scuffling sound behind the backdrop. An unseen hand clawed at it from behind and with a slithering and tearing noise it collapsed onto the stage in a cloud of dust. And, in the centre of all the mess, picking himself up gingerly, was Cedric. He peered down at the vicar in the front row, and the audience fell silent.

'I'm ever so sorry, vicar,' he said in a voice remarkably like the one that had been coming from the boxes, 'I think I tripped over all these thick socks you told me to wear.'

On Sunday afternoon, Jason and Jagdish were skimming stones down by the river.

'I wish I could think of something to do to Cedric,' said Jason, who was still sore from the pummelling his three friends had given him after the concert.

'What, for mucking up the trick?'

Jason threw another stone. 'Right,' he said, grimly.

'Well, what about the old Indian practical joke where you . . .' and, as Jagdish whispered, a smile spread across Jason's face. Life wasn't so bad, after all, he decided.

Jason and the Christmas Carol

It was December 1st, and it was starting to get dark as Jason, in football strip, got on his bike at the recreation ground by St Matthew's church hall.

The game had been a good one. St Matthew's church choir had beaten the Oakbridge Scouts two-nil—but, best of all, Cedric Stevens, the smallest choirboy, had been sat on by an exceedingly large Scout in the muddiest part of the pitch.

Jason puffed heavily up past the derelict black barn and reached the brow of the hill that led down to his house. Head down, he accelerated down the hill. He was swerving skilfully round familiar potholes when he saw, in the semi-darkness, a black shape lying across the road. He swerved, but it was too late. He hit the shape and somersaulted over the handlebars. His bike bounced and rattled away across the road, but, for Jason, everything went black and silent.

Then there swam inside his head a misty kaleidoscope of colours and shapes, darkness and light, silence and sounds. Through all this there came the sound of a voice, a long way away.

'Awake now?' it said. 'Awake now?'

'Wuff,' said Jason as he became fully conscious. What he had meant to say was 'Yes', but his tongue wouldn't work. The scene became sharper, and a face came into focus. It was Mr Jackson, the choirmaster at St Matthew's.

He hit the shape and somersaulted over the handlebars.

'You came off your bike! Old Man Davis found you in the middle of the road half an hour ago. You know where you are now?'

'Wuff-wuffle?' said Jason.

'Hospital—right first time. Mum will be here in a minute; Dad's just left and I'm here till she arrives. You've done something silly to your right leg, I gather.'

Jason ran his dry tongue round his mouth and tried to speak. 'Wha—what about the show?' he said. 'Can I still be in it? Shall I be better in time for it?'

'In time for what, young Jason?' said a nurse, coming up to his bed. Jason started to answer, but with a thermometer shoved into his mouth this was difficult.

Adrian Jackson spoke for him. 'It's a Christmas event at St Matthew's. We're calling it "The Christmas Carol"—a sort of musical, all about Christmas carols and how they began. Jason's the narrator and he was just wondering if he'll be better in time for it.'

'Well, we'll have to wait and see, sha'n't we!' said the nurse. Jason scowled at her over the thermometer. But then she smiled and sat on the bed. 'How *did* they begin?'

The choirmaster gave Jason a reassuring wink and said, 'Well, it all starts with the word itself; "carole" is an old French word—with an "e" on the end—which meant "to dance in a ring". In the thirteenth, fourteenth and fifteenth centuries it was a round dance, something like "Ring a ring of roses" in this country. Nothing to do with Christ's birth; in fact, they were quite pagan—no connection with God.'

'Fancy that,' said the nurse, taking the thermometer out of Jason's mouth and examining it. 'Well, I must be off.' As she went, Jason's mother came in and the choirmaster fished in his case and brought out a paper bag.

'Look, Jason,' he said. 'I've brought you some sweets and things. I'll slip them in this drawer for you—and mind, only one in the mornings and one in the afternoons!' He pulled open the drawer in the white bedside table, dropped the bag of sweets inside and shut the drawer.

Jason was to remember that simple action with some anguish before long.

☆ ☆ ☆

St Matthew's choir vestry was a hubbub of noise. Mr Jackson came in, but the noise went on for half a minute.

'Thank you. Good evening, everyone. Until now, we've been rehearsing THE CHRISTMAS CAROL in bits and pieces. Tonight I want to spend five minutes chatting with you, putting all the pieces together.'

He looked across at Cedric who was fishing about under his chair. The small choirboy looked up, red-faced from bending. 'Sir, it's my gerbil, sir! I brought him in my pocket and he's jumped out and I think he's sunk without trace!'

There was instant chaos as boys dived under their chairs to find it. A yell of delight came from the far end of the room when the head boy discovered it eating its way through Page One of *The Angel Gabriel.* With the gerbil back in Cedric's pocket, happy but hungry, and with Cedric warned never to bring it to choir practice again, Mr Jackson continued.

'In medieval days—say between AD 1000 and 1500—the words of carols were pagan, and often not very respectable! But the ones we're singing at the start of the show *are*; they may be silly, but quite respectable!'

'My gerbil's tickling me,' announced Cedric. The choirmaster pretended not to hear.

'Then we find the Christian Church beginning to adapt these pagan songs to Christian themes and Christian festivals—and not just Christmas, but Easter, Whitsun and so on.'

'Were they in English?' asked someone on Cantoris.

'Not all of them. A lot were macaronic—that is, in two languages, usually Latin and English. So the next carol in the show will be one of the earliest of these Christian versions, "The Cherry Tree Carol". You'll be monks in this one, carrying a silver cross on a pole.

'Then we move on to the fifteenth century proper, when the carol began to be far more musical. It might start with a passage for two soloists—called a "burden" or "chorus"—then the choir would come in, then the burden again, and so on. Melody and rhythm were the main ingredients in the fifteenth century and we're doing "The Boar's Head Carol" to illustrate it.

'That brings us to the sixteenth century, and we're singing a chirpy little number written by King Henry VIII, "Green Groweth the Holly"—typical of that period. By this time most carols were in duple or two-beat rhythm. Right, now let's sing all the carols I've talked about. We'll sing the rest later.'

☆ ☆ ☆

Jason was really fed up. He had just been told he had to stay in hospital over Christmas. There was something called a 'complication'. So now, to cap it all, someone else would be taking his part as narrator in the show. It wasn't fair, he told himself. It just was not fair. Narrator! In a Time Lord costume! And now he couldn't do it. Grumpily, he found himself looking round the ward. He looked at the other occupants, one by one. That was Andrew. He was sixteen, and he'd had his leg amputated. Rashid was twelve and had a broken back. Jason's eyes went from bed to bed, and as they completed a full circuit and came back to himself an idea went off with a crackling sound inside his head. Excited, he opened the little white drawer and rewarded himself with a bit of Mr Jackson's chocolate.

☆ ☆ ☆

The night of 'The Christmas Carol' came and went. The next day was Sunday and Jason had visits from some of the other choirboys and their parents with the news of the show and how it went off. The word 'terrific' seemed to sum it up.

The 21st came and went very, very slowly. The next morning dragged on and on. But at last it was almost six o'clock in the evening and Jason's brilliant idea was about to happen. A nurse helped him into a wheelchair and wheeled him into position.

In 1900, when Oakchester General Hospital was built, hospital wards were designed to hold about thirty beds ranged round the four walls. It was because Jason's ward was so big that the arrival of nineteen choirboys, one choirmaster, one guitarist and two large loudspeakers did not create a great deal of chaos. A little, but not much. There was a bustling, a shifting of beds and connecting of cables, the erection of screens and a rustling of crêpe paper behind them. There were visiting patients from other wards, and chairs to sit them in. Jason watched all this from his wheelchair with great satisfaction. His idea was actually happening.

Mr Jackson stepped over to a microphone.

'Ladies and gentlemen,' he began. 'A little while ago Jason Webb—just over there—fell off his bike and hurt his leg rather badly. It meant that he wasn't able to take his part in a church concert for which he had been practising for some time. But he had the bright idea of asking if I would bring the whole cast of choirboys here to put on the same show for all of you. Well, here we are. The show is all about Christmas carols and how they began. But first, here is your narrator with a special announcement.'

Jason wriggled into a more comfortable position in his wheelchair as his friend Spud, crackling and tinkling in what should have been Jason's Time Lord costume, came to the microphone.

'Hullo, everyone,' he said. 'Tonight we all want to tell Jason how sorry we are that he couldn't do his part at the show on Saturday.' Jason felt himself going red. 'And now, we've got a surprise for him, because . . .' he started to take off his silver foil helmet—'I should like him to take over the part of narrator this evening!'

Within seconds Jason was being dressed up in silver foil cape and helmet. He was so overcome with fright and embarrassment that he could barely see straight. Mr Jackson was bending over him, handing him the script. 'I'll just tap your shoulder as a cue to start each bit,' he said. The microphone was put close to his lips and the guitar began the bright little overture that Jason had heard so often in rehearsals.

The choirmaster tapped his shoulder. He heard his voice echoing round the big ward and gradually he found himself getting into the part of Time Lord. He glanced at the patients; their rapt attention told him he was doing well. Around him, medieval peasants danced in a ring; black-cloaked monks moved solemnly to the accompaniment of rustling black crêpe paper. Six carols had been sung and the story had reached the eighteenth century.

'At the time of the Reformation,' he went on, 'the Roman Catholic church was going through a time of total change. This led to a completely new branch of the Church springing up—it was called the Protestant Church. There were a lot of big differences between the two, and because Christmas carols had been so much a Roman Catholic tradition in the past, the Protestants would not allow them to be sung. So, for the next hundred years or so, carols were not sung at all. Of course, this meant that people gradually forgot them altogether. But then, almost into the 1700s, a wonderful new carol was born—"While shepherds watched their flocks by night"'.

A group of singers emerged from behind the screens, carrying lanterns and dressed in long coats and tall hats. Jason got a fit of the giggles when he saw Cedric dressed as a small girl in long golden curls and a bright green ankle-length dress. But they all sang the old carol with enthusiasm—patients, visitors and choirboys together.

'About sixty or so years later, in 1760, the Christmas carol really began to flourish. People liked them and kept wanting more. It was then that Charles Wesley wrote "Hark, the herald angels sing", and new ones kept coming for a hundred years, when "O little town of Bethlehem" turned up and became a favourite.'

A solo chorister appeared in front of the screens and, unaccompanied, sang the first verse of that simple carol. Then the choir completed it.

'But the original dance-like carol,' continued Jason, 'was disappearing. Carols became more like hymns. In recent years composers and writers have discovered a lot of these old dancing and lullaby carols from all over Europe—like this next one—as well as writing a lot of new ones.'

The show drew to an end, with a speech from the supervisor and long, loud applause. The visitors began to leave, the St Matthew's choirboys climbed into cars or trudged home along the lanes through the cold Christmassy night.

But among them a small child in a long green dress and flowing golden locks suddenly stopped.

'Dad!' My gerbil! I've left it in the hospital! When we went to see Jason before the show—I left it there. Quick—I must go and get it!'

'Oh, Cedric,' groaned his father. 'Where did you leave it, for goodness' sake?'

'Well, you know Jason's bed? It's got a sort of white table thing beside it, with a drawer in the top. I was going to ask him if I could put the gerbil in there during the show but then the nurse came and moved him before I could—so I just put it in.'

And it was at that very moment that Jason, who had just been put back to bed, was reaching into the little white drawer to reward himself with another piece of chocolate.

The ward resounded with a surprised yell.

Jason and the Epiphany Men

Jason had never ridden a camel before and he was amazed at how brilliantly he was riding it.

The motion was quite unlike that of a horse—which, thanks to Old Man Davis and his retired pony Bodger at the farm next door, he had learned to ride when he was quite small. The camel rolled and lurched; there were moments when he actually felt as if he was floating through the air. Very dream-like, he thought.

He was in Africa. Persia, to be exact. He had never been to Africa before, but, like riding the camel, he felt as if he had lived there all his life. The road was barely a road at all; just a track, winding across the dry, sandy desert in the blazing sunshine and taking him through the shade of occasional clumps of palm trees where there were sounds of conversation and water being drawn from wells.

There were three others travelling with him, each on his own camel, and now they stopped and drank the cold, clear water from a well and refreshed themselves with mouthfuls of sweet, succulent dates.

Minutes later, Jason and the three couriers were on their way again, heading for the Dead Sea. Riding tandem behind one of the men was a smaller boy—he had been told he was the man's nephew—who so far had not spoken to him. Jason had looked hard at him while they rested in the oasis, and he was sure he recognised him.

Now, as they rode on, he thought about his last sight of his mother and father, waving goodbye from the steps of their hotel, of his father calling out, 'See you at the Dead Sea, Jason!', and his mother reassuring him that he would be perfectly safe with the three couriers and that he would have that nice little boy for company. As he pictured them in his mind he told himself sharply that he was not feeling homesick.

The shadows of the sandhills were growing longer now, and the air was cooler. The blue sky was taking on a hint of purple and, as they approached the biggest oasis yet, there came on the breeze the most magical perfume of blossom that he had ever smelled.

They were to stop there for the night. One of the men helped him down from the saddle as the camel settled on its knees and he stood and stretched himself. The small boy came across to him, tossing a stick in the air and catching it.

'What's your name, anyway?' said the boy, scratching his back with the stick.

'Jason. What's yours?'

'Cedric.'

Jason almost choked with surprise. He nearly said, 'You can't be!', but he looked at the stick and decided the other boy might use it on him if he argued about his name. Instead, he said, 'Where do you come from?'

'Turkey,' said Cedric.

Jason wasn't quite sure where Turkey was, but just as he started twisting his question mark of hair—which he always did when he was not sure what to say next—the men called them to an enormous tent where the sounds of music and people having a good time spilled out onto the evening

The men were calling them to an enormous tent . . .

air. Once inside, the smells of good food were delicious. Jason's mouth watered.

☆ ☆ ☆

Jason and the Turkish boy came out of the tent half an hour later wiping their mouths. 'Leviticus! That was good!' said Jason.

Cedric (and Jason had to remind himself constantly that this was not the Cedric he knew) gave a short laugh.

'Call that good? You want to come to Turkey.'

Jason answered with a very regrettable but satisfactory burp. One of the men came out of the tent and called them.

'Follow me, young masters. I will show you where you are to sleep tonight—a beautiful tent all to yourselves. Then you are to come and sit by our camp fire for a while before you sleep, and we can talk of other things.'

☆ ☆ ☆

The fire was bright; the flames darted and the sparks crackled and flew up into the dark night. The little group of men and boys talked quietly as distant dogs barked and crickets chirrupped in the date palms. Jason looked up at the sky and thought that the stars had never looked brighter. They appeared to hang from the sky, as though you could put out your hand and pick them, like picking fruit from a tree.

'Well,' said one of the three men in a slow, deep voice, as if he were talking to himself, 'we are five travellers in the desert; each on a different mission. You, Jason, are our companion until we meet your mother and father at the hotel beyond the Dead Sea. They are brave, and fly in an aeroplane. We couriers prefer our camels. Our transport is slow, but from an aeroplane you cannot smell the Myrtle blossom!

'And you, Cedric; you are to go to your new school—an exciting journey indeed for one who is so young.

'But we three couriers; where are we bound? And why, you may ask, are we travelling to the west?' His dark eyes caught a reflection of the firelight as he looked at the boys. Then he glanced at the other two men, and they nodded, as though giving him permission to tell a secret.

'We are not all that we seem to be. We are not simply couriers, although we do carry important papers for others, and we are escorting you boys across the desert. No, we three are called Magi. We have special powers; we understand some of the mysteries of the stars. Ah! I see you are surprised! Yes, we are of the great Turanian tribe of Persia. Through the stars, we know things that ordinary people cannot know. We are like kings to our people, because of our powers.'

'What are your names, please?' said Jason, hoping that it was not bad manners.

The man who had been speaking raised his hand to indicate the other two. 'Here is Melchior, on my left, and on my right is Balthazar. I am called Gaspar.'

Cedric screwed up his face in puzzlement. 'Gaspar, Melchior and Balthazar? I thought that's what Father Christmas called his reindeer!'

'Shut up, you idiot!' said Jason. 'That's Donner, Blitzen, Prancer, and—and—'

Gaspar came to his rescue. 'I think I can help you,' he smiled, 'and at the same time I can show you one of my powers.'

Jason, who had been sitting cross-legged, fell backwards with surprise, for in front of his eyes like a huge TV screen came the full list of the reindeers' names, the letters gleaming in the darkness like silver on black velvet.

'Gosh!' said Jason.

'Crumbs!', said Cedric, who had just received the same picture.

'Don't be alarmed,' said Gaspar. 'Whenever you want to remember their names you will see my pretty silver words in front of your eyes.'

The vision faded, and Jason looked with new respect at his noble companions. It was Melchior's turn to speak.

'Our names are familiar to you because they were the names of the Three Wise Men who took gifts to the Christ Child. You will not find their names in the Bible, though, or that there were three of them, for it is only by word of mouth, by tradition, that the three names are remembered today.' He leaned forward and spoke quietly.

'How would you like to be transported back in time to the very year of the Epiphany itself, when the Christ was revealed to the Magi?'

And Cedric, before Jason could stop him, jumped up and yelled, 'Yeah! Yeah!'

Instantly, Jason found himself in another saddle, on a different camel, riding under the stars with Melchior, Gaspar and Balthazar. Other things had changed, too.

Instead of the new lightweight jacket and trousers which his mother had bought for him in London, he was now wearing a strange linen tunic with a leather belt at the waist. Flung over his shoulders was a heavy goatskin cape, tucked down into his belt to keep it in place. He was glad of its warmth; the desert was cold.

The other three camels were ahead, carrying the three men and Cedric, whose arms were clinging round the waist of his uncle Gaspar.

Jason looked up into this other sky, two thousand years younger than the one he had seen above the camp fire. Without surprise he saw, directly ahead of them, an enormous star. It gleamed and twinked like a diamond, its colour shifting through the spectrum as he swung and rocked in the saddle.

The group was slowing down, for an oasis—a big one—was appearing out of the darkness. Oil lamps flickered through the trees, women with tiny children moved about by the well, camels stirred sleepily at their tethering posts. The five travellers dismounted. Jason leaped from his saddle unaided, landing in the warm, deep sand before his camel had finished kneeling.

'What's in those boxes?' he asked Balthazar as they huddled together round a fire with half a dozen other people, and he pointed to three highly decorated caskets that lay at the man's side. Balthazar looked at his two companions, questioning, and they both nodded, smiling. He drew one box towards him. Jason, his mouth full of fig cake, leaned over to watch him open it. Cedric came galloping round behind the group and fell to his knees, excited. 'Is it food?' he asked.

The flames flashed in the gilt paintwork on the box as the lid was opened. Balthazar put his hand inside and drew it out, fist closed. He stretched out his arm toward the boys and slowly opened his hand. In his palm lay a single large gold coin, smooth with age and glinting as only pure gold can. 'It is gold, for a king,' he said. 'It will show him that we know he is a king though the world will not recognise his kingship.'

As Gaspar opened his own box he smiled. 'My gift is not as beautiful to look at, but just wait till I drop some on the fire,' and he tipped a small brass jar until a thin trickle of liquid gum flowed down on to red embers on the edge of the fire. There wafted up to their faces the most nose-wrinkling perfume, half sweet, half bitter. 'This is pure incense—frankincense—to show the king that we know that he is also God.'

Melchior was opening his casket now and both boys craned their necks to see what came out. Disappointingly, it was nothing but a handful of dry, herb-like flakes. 'Sweet-smelling myrrh, for embalming the dead,' said Melchior softly. 'It will show him that we know he will be a man of many sorrows, though his death will bring new life.'

All this talk about a king—and a very strange one at that—made Jason feel strangely sad yet excited. 'But who is this king? And why does he need to be told these things?' He felt a tight feeling growing in his throat at the thought of these mysteries.

'His name is Jesus,' said all three men at once, as though it were a solemn creed which they were used to saying together. 'Jesus' was a common name among the boys and men. Yet the way the men said the name of this king made it sound tragic. Tragic and majestic.

'Now, you must look into the fire,' said Balthazar. Both boys did as they were told, but something made Jason see the flames through starting tears.

As they looked, the fire slowly changed shape and it became the camp fire of two thousand years later. The three men were rising. 'Time for sleeping, boys!' said Balthazar. 'We want you to look refreshed when you meet your parents at the airport, Jason—and when you reach your school, Cedric.'

On his thin mattress, Jason lay thinking for a long time. The animal-skin bed covers were light but warm. Cedric was soon asleep, muttering to himself occasionally and kicking Jason as he dreamed. Then sleep came to Jason, too, and the sounds of the night faded into his dreams.

A loud buzzing woke him. He sat up in bed. The sun was streaming down on him. He rubbed his eyes and switched off his alarm clock. His duvet had slipped off the bed on to the floor. The tent was bigger than he had remembered it. Its walls were square, and there was a white ceiling. From somewhere a long way below his bed there was the sound of letters being shoved through a letterbox. Someone was whistling outside.

His hand, propping him up, felt the corner of something hard sticking out from under his pillow. It was a book. He started at the cover. *In the Tracks of the Magi*, it said. Yes, he thought. It was a good book—he'd been reading it by the light of his torch last night. Great story. Funny, though. He had the feeling he'd actually been there, out in the desert . . . He shook the sleep out of his head and told himself not to be stupid.

In spite of his stiff leg, he beat his sister Cecilia into the bathroom by exactly two seconds.

Jason and the Ashes

It was the afternoon of Ash Wednesday and Jason was in deep trouble. It all began on the previous Sunday after Morning Prayer at St Matthew's. Mr Jackson, the choirmaster, had called Jason while he was disrobing.

'Jason,' he said, reaching into a cardboard box on top of the vestry piano and holding up a stack of sealed white envelopes, 'you said the other day that your newspaper round takes you to nearly all of the choirboys' homes. Now, would you be kind enough to deliver these, with the papers, tomorrow morning?'

Jason nodded. 'Yes—OK. But couldn't the boys have taken them home just now, after the services?'

'They could, yes—but the last time I gave them letters to take home half the parents never got them. This letter is very important and I want to be quite sure that every parent gets it tomorrow morning. THAT-IS-MOST-IMPORTANT,' he said slowly, emphasising each word with a gentle prod at Jason's chest.

'Don't worry,' he laughed, 'the letters'll be there by seven o'clock tomorrow morning—promise!'

He had fastened the cardboard box on to his carrier rack and pedalled importantly home, parking his bike in the shed and putting the boxful of letters on the bench, ready for the morning.

Now, three days later, it was after school on Ash Wednesday afternoon, and Jason was in deep trouble. He knew it the moment he walked into the shed to get on with

He knew it the moment he walked into the shed . . .

repainting his skateboard. For there, on the bench, half covered by an old newspaper, was the boxful of letters.

☆ ☆ ☆

That evening, Cedric was in the bath and he was singing his version of the latest hit. Cedric had two styles of singing. One was kept for the choir, when he produced a quite pleasant sound. The other was wide-ranging in its volume and terrifying in its tone. Cats jumped when he started; dogs howled.

Suddenly, he stopped, remembering something. He sat up, blew the froth away from his chest (he had spilt half the bottle of bubble bath into the water) and took from the chair a copy of 'Lord, let me know mine end' lent to him reluctantly by Mr Jackson in order to get one difficult passage right. Holding it well above the white foam rising all round him he began to sing—in the choir mode.

Mrs Stevens, downstairs doing the ironing, smiled. She began to reflect on her dear little son. How talented! A piercing yell from the bathroom made her drop the iron on her foot. As she hopped round in circles unable to decide whether to nurse her foot or pick up the iron, which was beginning to scorch the rug, there was a damp sort of thudding down the stairs and the door opened. Smothered in foam and staring at her through eye holes, Cedric looked like a terrified snow-man. He held up a sodden copy of 'Lord, let me know mine end'.

'Mum! I dropped it in the bath! Mr Jackson'll KILL me!'

Mrs Stevens had sorted out her priorities and was now rubbing her foot. 'I shouldn't be at all surprised,' she said. 'Let me know the time and place of execution.'

☆ ☆ ☆

Jason could not move. He stared at the boxful of envelopes. The box stared back at him. He backed away and went slowly in a daze down the side passage to the front gate, scratching his head and twisting his tuft of hair. Then, sticking his hands deep into his pockets he wandered down the lane, staring at the ground and seeing nothing but that boxful of letters. He had let Mr Jackson down. He was no longer trustworthy. He rounded the bend in the lane. He saw a stone and kicked it viciously. It was a good goal kick; the stone rose high in the air and cracked down on to the tarmac a good fifteen metres ahead, bounding along and coming to rest at the feet of a man who was emerging from farm gates.

The man stopped and looked at him. 'Hullo, Jason,' he smiled. 'What's up?'

'Oh, hullo Mr Davis.' Jason forced a smile for his old friend. 'Er—nothing, really.'

Old Man Davis, as everyone in Oakbridge called him, sat down on the barrow he had been wheeling. He reached into a loaded sack, felt among the straw and brought out an apple, holding it out to Jason. 'Whenever someone adds that word "really" they usually mean "something". Have an apple.' The sun came out from behind heavy February clouds and Jason began to feel better.

'Thank you. Well,' Jason bit into the apple and chewed for a moment. Then he said, 'Um,' and twisted his hair almost into a corkscrew. He took another bite. Old Man Davis waited patiently.

'Well, the thing is this—' and Jason poured out the whole story. His friend listened without interrupting until the story ended. Then he said, 'And is there anything I can do to help?' He worked on the principle that nobody wanted your advice unless they asked for it.

'What d'you think I should do?' said Jason.

'All I can do is to tell you what I would do in your place. What you actually do is for you to decide. As for me, I would go and deliver the letters as fast as possible, then I'd go immediately to Mr Jackson and tell him what's happened. And, of course, apologise.'

'But he'll murder me!'

'I doubt it.' Mr Davis stood up. 'He'll think all the more of you for owning up, especially if he can see you're really repentant. After all, it is Ash Wednesday today.'

'Ash Wednesday, yes. I've never understood about Ash Wednesday—what it's all about. Anyway, I'll go and do the letters now, and then—Oh, Leviticus!'—he covered his eyes as he thought about the prospect—'I'll go and see Mr Jackson. Well, thanks a lot, Mr Davis!'

'Don't mention it. And if you want to know more about Ash Wednesday,' he called after Jason's rapidly disappearing figure, 'drop in any time!'

☆ ☆ ☆

Jason's newly-mended leg protested as he pedalled furiously up the street delivering the letters. He tore back along the lane toward St Matthew's Church and Mr Jackson's flat just opposite. He thumped the door knocker and rang the bell. Then he rang the bell and thumped the knocker. Then he did both together. But there was no answer.

The next-door neighbour put her head out of a window and asked who it was. Jason told her, and was told in reply that Mr Jackson would be away until Friday choir practice.

At supper that evening, Jason said as casually as he could, 'Oh, Mum, by the way, what was Mr Jackson's letter all about—the one I left on the sideboard?'

Mrs Webb put down her knife and fork and looked him in the eye. 'At last!' she said. 'I've been wondering when you would bring that subject up. Now, when were you supposed to have given me that letter, may I ask?'

☆ ☆ ☆

The following afternoon Jason took Old Man Davis at his word and, having told his mother where he would be, called in to the farm after school. With a large cream bun facing oblivion between his teeth and a cup of tea at his side, he watched Mr Davis settling himself opposite in his deep armchair.

'So you won't be able to confess to Mr Jackson until tomorrow's choir practice, then?'

Jason shook his head, and when he could manage it he said, 'And I'm really, really miserable'.

'H'm. Funny you should use that word "miserable". Did you know it comes from a word that means "have mercy!" or "pity me!"? It's a Latin word—miserere. And I imagine mercy is just what Mr Jackson will have when you confess!'

'Certainly hope so,' said Jason.

'Ash Wednesday,' mused the man. 'How would you fancy smothering yourself in cold ashes from the garden bonfire and dressing up in old sacks? That's where Ash Wednesday began. The Hebrew people, in Old Testament times, would show their real sorrow for being sinful—disobeying God's laws—by doing just that. Before they went into the temple to repent of their sin, they would dress in the roughest, poorest possible cloth, called sackcloth, and pour ashes all over their head. It was a sign that they realised they were really unworthy of God's grace and forgiveness. Then they would go in and ask for God's mercy on them, and to forgive them.'

Jason, with a blob of cream on the tip of his nose, said, 'So "being sorry" means being really miserable about what we've done wrong?' Mr Davis nodded, and Mrs Davis, who had come into the room while they were talking, said, 'That's right—and now my father-in-law is going to put on sackcloth and ashes and explain to me just what he means by cleaning his boots on my nice clean kitchen floor!'

At school next morning, during break, Jason saw Cedric coming up to him. 'Hey!' called Cedric. 'Something awful's happened. I dropped "Lord, let me know mine end" in the bath and it's ruined and Mr Jackson's going to kill me when he finds out!'

'I shouldn't be surprised,' said Jason, heartlessly.

'Pig!', said Cedric. 'He'll probably do it at choir practice tonight.'

A brilliant idea came into Jason's head. 'I say, *when* did you drop it in the bath—which day?'

'Wednesday—why?'

'That was Ash Wednesday! Leviticus! You know what you've got to do now, don't you? You've got to apologise dressed in sackcloth and with ashes all over your head. It's a rule at St Matthews—isn't it?' he said to his friend John who had just joined them. John nodded.

'Don't worry, it's quite simple,' said Jason, his arm round Cedric's shoulder. 'All you do is to get an old sack, cut a hole in the bottom for your head, then put it on upside-down and poke your head through the hole. Then you get some cold ashes from any old fire and pour some over your head.'

The bell rang, and break was over. Cedric, looking worried, walked into school very, very slowly.

☆ ☆ ☆

When Mr Jackson went into the choir vestry that evening he found Jason there, early and alone.

'Hullo, Jason!' he smiled. Then, as he saw the look on Jason's face, he added, 'what's wrong?'

The whole story came out, Jason speaking in a very croaky voice. When he had finished, the choirmaster started playing random chords, quietly.

'There are a lot of people who don't really understand what confession and repentance mean,' he said, slowly, looking at the keyboard as he played. 'But you do, now. And although you did not actually commit a sin—except, possibly, of carelessness—you've gone through a kind of hell, haven't you? And when we confess our sin to God, our pride, selfishness, cheating, and so on, that's just how we should feel—a kind of hell. We should cry out for God's mercy, because our sin has actually hurt him. But how often do we feel like that when we confess to God? How often do I?' he added, softly. Then he stopped playing and turned to look at Jason. He was smiling. 'Listen,' he said.

'Last Monday morning, just before I went away for the week, I thought I would make a spot-check to see that you had remembered to deliver those letters. You see, it was particularly important to me that they were delivered that morning, before parents heard my news through gossip.'

'About you getting engaged—yes, Mum told me.'

'Exactly. People like to be told personally rather than

getting it secondhand. Well, I decided to ring up one of the parents to see if they had received the letter. They hadn't. Then I rang someone else. They hadn't, either. So I knew you had forgotten. Then I rang every one of the twenty parents with my news and explained about the letter. But I decided not to tell you—I felt that the lesson would be good for you. You would have every right to be cross with me about that.'

'No—oh, no. I mean, it's taught me about confession, and Ash Wednesday, and all that. And I'm very sorry.'

'Forgiven and forgotten!' said the choirmaster. There was a thundering of feet in the passage. The door burst open; Friday evening choir practice was under way.

They were about to begin the first piece when the door opened slowly and a small sack entered the room, topped by the head of Cedric Stevens, covered in grey ash. A roar of laughter began, but the choirmaster held up his hand and silence was retrieved.

Jason was astonished—surely Cedric hadn't actually believed him?

Mr Jackson called Cedric to stand in front of the choir and tell them what had happened.

'Well,' said Cedric, 'you see I phoned Mr Jackson this afternoon because I'd dropped some music in the bath and then I told him that someone said I'd got to put on sackcloth and ashes and I asked him if that was right and he said No it wasn't but would I mind dressing up anyway to help him do a talk this evening about Ash Wednesday—and, well, here I am.'

Cedric got Jason in his sights and beamed him the most irritating, charming smile that he could manage.

Jason and the Procession of Palms

It was a Saturday afternoon toward the end of March. Jason and three other St Matthew's choirboys, Spud, John and Henry, pedalled hard toward the city of Oakchester for a shopping expedition. They had just named themselves 'The Summit Club.'

The purpose of The Summit Club was serious discussion, and all really important meetings would involve a 'banquet'. Today, following the rules they had made the previous day, each had taken exactly £1 from his savings to buy his own food. There were three items; a main course (to be cooked over a fire), a pudding and a drink. The shopping finished, they rode back along the lanes toward Oakbridge —but not home. Because the banquet had to be prepared, cooked and eaten in the old black derelict barn that stood in the meadow between St Matthew's Church and the village.

The very first Summit Club banquet this Saturday afternoon was a slightly nervous one. The four of them had been asked to present a five-minute drama about Palm Sunday for the Family Service at St Matthew's on Palm Sunday morning. That was the following Sunday and, so far, nothing had been prepared.

☆ ☆ ☆

While The Summit Club were happily preparing their banquet, Cedric, who was too young and much too troublesome to be a member, was bored. Bored and irritable. His mother had got so tired of his wandering round the house, opening and shutting doors, chasing Boggles the cat and teasing Gerald the Gerbil that she had shooed him out of the house. He stood looking at his old bike. Then he got on it, pushed off down the side passage and rode along the village street.

An idea came. He knew what he would do. He would go and inspect his secret hoard of treasure. It was in the safest place in the world, where no-one would ever find it. It was up a ladder, across a dark, wooden floor, and hidden in a wooden box under a pile of hay. It was, in fact, in the loft of the old, black, derelict barn on the road to St Matthew's.

☆ ☆ ☆

A haze of blue smoke drifted up into the fading afternoon light above the barn. Four boys sat on old wooden boxes, crowding round a very healthy-looking camp fire. The fire had been made in the middle of a weed-covered brick floor just outside the old doors—or, rather, where the doors had once been before some forgotten storm had wrenched them from their hinges. In the best Scouts' tradition, two crossed poles stood at each side of the fire, with a transverse pole running between them, and from this hung two pans, one for soup and one for sausages and bacon.

Bread and margarine was permissible by special decree in these banquets, and John was busy spreading margarine on a growing pile of bread.

'Bread's all ready,' he called to Jason, who was hopping round in small circles having just splashed hot fat on his thumb, 'how's the cooking?'

☆ ☆ ☆

The meal was over. The sun was low, now, and beginning to turn the sky in the west to a soft, pink-and-orange glow. The four boys crouched round the fire, talking earnestly.

'Look,' said Jason. 'It all begins with Jesus telling two of his disciples to go to the village outside Jerusalem and they'll see a colt tied up there.'

'Actually,' said John, 'he said it was a colt that no-one had ever ridden before.'

Spud looked up from the bit of wood he was trying to light from the hot ash. 'Yes, but we can't actually show that, can we.'

'We can't show the colt, anyway!' said Henry.

'Hey, what about using Bonzo!' said Spud. Bonzo was his very own dog—a black terrier with a white tail.

'Don't be pathetic!' said Jason and Henry together. Henry said, 'Can't you hear them all laughing when we try and pretend it's a donkey?'

'Colt,' said John.

'Same thing,' said Jason. 'Colt and donkey mean the same thing.'

'Actually,' said John, 'colt means a horse, pony, donkey or ass under four years old. I looked it up. This one was a baby ass so it's called a colt.'

'All right, all right,' said Jason, who knew from experience that John was usually right about words. 'Forget what it's called. Forget having it. We've already decided that we're just going to tell the story, but from four points of view.'

'Well, let's decide who's going to be who,' said Henry.

'Whom,' said John softly.

Jason intervened. 'How about Spud being one of the disciples who gets the colt, Henry and John being people in the crowd who describe what they can see, and I'll be Jesus,' he said.

Three loud howls of ridicule rang round the empty barn behind them. Mysteriously, a wisp of hay was dislodged from the loft and it floated down into the doorway. But none of the four noticed it.

'Ho, yes!' said Spud. 'Jason will have the plum part, won't he!', and the other two joined in. When they had finished, John said, 'Well, let's be fair, he's the best actor, and you've got to have someone pretty good to take the part of Jesus. I vote Jason does it. All in favour?'

Jason was uncomfortable about the way he had volunteered to take the part. He began to apologise, but, as if he had never spoken, John went on, 'So that's fixed. Now, Jason starts off, telling the congregation who he is—Jesus.'

'Yes,' said Henry, 'and then Spud describes how Jesus asked him and his friend to go and find the colt and then how he found it and had to explain to the people standing by why he was taking it—'

Spud broke in. 'But I think Jesus should say first that *the people would ask* why the colt was being taken away. That's what it says in the gospel.'

They agreed about that. The story gradually took shape. Henry would represent the crowd, talking about how they had heard about Jesus being the great new King of the Jews, and about how he was going to ride into Jerusalem; how they had collected branches of palm trees with all their neighbours, ready to greet him in the traditional way for a King.

Then the disciple would describe the scene as he followed Jesus, the street lined down both sides with an enormous, excited crowd of people, all shouting 'Hosanna in the highest! Blessed is he who comes in the name of the Lord. Blessed is the coming kingdom of our father David!'

John discovered a bit of sausage stuck to the side of the pan and nibbled at it. 'What about the bad bit that comes later—the mob all screaming at him and saying he'd got to be crucified?'

'I s'pose we've *got* to have that as well?' said Jason. It was that part of the story, the crucifixion and death of Jesus, that always made him feel bad, almost as if he had been one of the crowd shouting for Jesus to be crucified. The scene was always so real when he thought about it.

Henry was talking. 'So, is that OK, then?'

☆ ☆ ☆

Cedric had arrived at the barn half an hour ago. Delighted to find The Summit Club there, and even more pleased that they had not a clue of his presence, he crept round the back of the barn, through the big gap in the wooden planking, across the floor and up the ladder to the loft. Lying flat on his stomach he could see them. And he could hear every word.

He went quietly to his secret box, lifted the hay that covered it and there were his treasures. Eleven snails' shells. He picked them up, one by one, and examined them. He liked the spiral patterns; each one was different. He pretended that they were ancient, magic fossils that in response to a curious spell would turn into dragons and go rampaging across the countryside, eating teachers, dentists and all boys bigger than himself. He put them carefully back in the box, covered it with hay and crept to where he could both

Cedric's round face wrinkled into the terrible expression which always signalled a plot.

see and hear The Summit Club. They were in the middle of discussing the problem about the colt and how they could represent it. Cedric's round face wrinkled into the terrible expression which always signalled a plot. He listened for only another few seconds, then, silently (for Cedric), he climbed down the ladder and raced back to his bike.

'So,' he whispered to himself as he pedalled homewards, 'it's impossible to have a colt in the play, is it?'

☆ ☆ ☆

The Palm Sunday congregation was large. The singing was lusty, and the vicar beamed out at his flock as they sat down at the end of the second hymn. He was happy, he told them, to be able to announce a special presentation of the Palm Sunday story by four of the choirboys.

Out came Jason, dressed in Middle-Eastern robes, and began to tell the congregation about who he was, what he had been doing among the people, and why he had come from God the Father to preach, teach and heal. Many of the people, he said, thought he was going to be an earthly king. To help them to understand his real mission, he was about to ride into Jerusalem on a young colt—the Hebrew prophets, he said, had foretold this hundreds of years before. At this point, Jason walked away and Spud came on, dressed in a long, rough piece of cloth wrapped round his waist and flung over his shoulder.

'I'm a fisherman—or I was until I started following Jesus,' he began, and went on to tell how Jesus had told him and one of his friends to go to a certain spot, where he would find a young colt tied up. 'So that's what we did,' he ended.

He went to the curtained door on the north side of the church and disappeared behind the curtain. At this point there was a sudden buzz of excited chatter among the congregation, for from behind the choirstalls there came, slowly and awkwardly, a donkey. Or, rather, a pantomime donkey, whose front and hind legs were obviously those of two small boys. It wobbled toward the middle of the chancel steps, and stopped.

John and Spud emerged from behind the curtain, talking loudly to each other.

'I don't see how Jesus could possibly have known that there would be a young colt waiting for us,' said John.

'No, neither do I. But Jesus has done some extraordinary things while we've been with him. I don't think this would be impossible for him. I wouldn't be at all surprised—' Spud stopped, and stared at the donkey. 'I—I—' he stammered.

'W—w—w—' said John, gazing in disbelief.

'Get on with it!' hissed the donkey. 'It's us, Cedric and Roger. Lead us over to Jason.'

With remarkable presence of mind, Spud ad-libbed, 'Well, we should have known Jesus knew what he was talking about' and gave the donkey a very satisfying whack on its rump.

☆ ☆ ☆

In the choir vestry half an hour later, Jason, Spud, Henry and John were standing round Cedric and shouting at him. In the middle of a long and terrifying speech by Jason, Mr Jackson came in.

'OK, calm down, Jason,' he said. 'Let's sit down and talk about it.' He went and sat on his piano stool and when they were quiet, he smiled round at them.

'Quite by accident I discovered Cedric's and Roger's little

plot to surprise us all by coming in dressed up in the Christmas Panto donkey outfit. I honestly don't think they would have gone through with it, mind you. But when they told me about it I decided it might not be a bad idea. I knew you would be surprised to find it there, and I felt it would add to the realism—because I'm quite sure those two disciples were surprised, too. So Cedric and Roger had strict instructions to come on, then tell you to lead them off toward Jason and then out of sight, so that Henry could come straight on and talk about what actually happened —from the crowd's point of view. And I can tell you,' he grinned, 'that six people came up to me after the service was over just now and said how brilliant the whole thing was—and how they had enjoyed seeing the donkey!'

'Colt, sir,' said Spud.

'Ass's colt,' said Jason.

'A young ass,' said Henry.

'A horse, pony, donkey or ass under four years old,' said John.

'Precisely,' said the choirmaster. 'Well, everyone happy? I do hope so, because this afternoon you're all invited to my house for tea—and it's cream buns.'

And at four o'clock there were some twenty boys standing round the kitchen table, each with an earnest expression and bulging cheeks. However, the expression on Cedric's and Roger's face was easier to imagine than to see, for each had just had two very creamy cream buns pushed into their faces. Mr Jackson noticed the event but decided that he would not interfere.

It was obviously a private matter.

Jason and the Easter Holiday

'Jason, have you written that letter to Aunt Mary yet? You know it's got to be posted tonight—we've got to be at the airport by six in the morning so there won't be time tomorrow.'

'Nearly finished it, Mum', called Jason from his room. He scanned the page he had already written.

Dear Aunt Mary,

Thank you very much for my birthday present. Socks are very useful, specially grey ones. How are you? It's quite sunny today. Tomorrow we are all getting up at five and going to Jerusalem by air. It is quite sunny there, too. Now it is raining. Cedric is coming, too, worse luck.

He decided that he'd written enough and added 'Your affectionate nephew, Jason.' Then he said, 'Grey socks! Huh!' He sealed the envelope and (to make sure it was sealed, he told himself) gave it six very hefty thumps with his fist, rattling everything on his table.

'Jason! What on earth are you doing?'

'Saying thanks to Aunt Mary,' called Jason, 'for the six pairs of super grey socks.'

☆ ☆ ☆

The following morning at twenty-five past nine Jason felt as if someone had poured warm treacle in his ears. It was making little popping sounds in his head. Their flight had just taken off and the cabin was pressurising. It was his first flight in a passenger aircraft. He looked out of his window at the ground. Grey clouds below were slowly thickening as the aircraft climbed higher, and all the countryside was disappearing. Finally, it was gone. He swallowed, and his ears popped again. He looked through the gap in the headrests but all he could see of his sister Cecilia was her hand on her arm-rest. A sharp elbow dug into his lap as the small boy next to him leaned across to see out of the window.

'It's all right, there's nothing to see,' said Jason. 'You're lucky—when you get your turn at the window seat we'll be landing, and it's bound to be clear at Amman airport.'

Cedric sighed. 'Oh, I wasn't looking for the ground,' he said, flopping back into his seat, 'I was looking to see if there were any birds getting sucked into the engines.'

'Cedric!' said his father from the next seat.

'Cedric, *really*!' said his mother from the next seat but one. Then she leaned across her husband to look Cedric straight between the eyes, wagging her finger at him. 'Now, you just listen to me—this is Easter-time, a time of peace and joy. We are going to the Holy Land to see where Jesus lived. We've saved up for this holiday with the Webbs *and it is going to be a happy and peaceful Easter holiday*. Now, we expect you to behave like an ordinary, decent boy, and we don't want any of your nasty tricks or horrid talk about—well, just behave yourself. Do you understand?'

Cedric smiled and said, 'Of course, Mum!' so sweetly that his mother relented and returned his smile.

Jason, on the other hand, was preparing himself for the worst.

☆ ☆ ☆

There ensued a brief skirmish.

Sunshine woke him the next morning. Sunshine, and the sound of birds singing and waves breaking on a shore. His dreams merged slowly into reality and he sat up. He craned his neck to look out of the hotel bedroom window. So this was Galilee! In the other bed Cedric lay flat on his back, mouth open, and snoring gently. Jason knew exactly what he had to do and wasted no time. He slid out of bed and tiptoed across the room to the washbasin. Running the cold water on to his face-flannel until it was soaked he turned and held it over Cedric's open mouth. He scored a direct hit on the gap between his front teeth. Cedric spluttered, snorted loudly, sat up and jumped out of bed. Jason was doubled up with laughter but by the time Cedric reached him he was rolled up tightly in his bedclothes. There ensued a brief skirmish during which pyjama trousers were wrenched off, water was splashed liberally all over the hotel bedroom and one glass tumbler smashed in the wash-basin.

Their punishment was to go together to the hotel manager and ask how much they owed him for the tumbler. Sternly, the manager told them. When they returned with the money he thanked them and told them to follow him to the front entrance.

Then he put his arms round both boys' shoulders and, looking out across the water, he said, 'Over there—you see those men throwing a fishing-net from a boat? That's just the kind of boat Jesus of Nazareth used when he went on this lake with his friends and then stood and preached to the people here on the shore. Now, if you want to you can hire a boat like that and go fishing. And this,' he said, pressing the money for the broken glass back into Jason's hand, 'will help pay for the trip.'

'Thanks—thanks ever so much,' they said, together.

'You've apologised, I've forgiven you. It's called "loving your neighbour". Have a happy day!' He went back to his office.

Jason looked out across the water. 'Swim?' he said.

'Yeah!' said Cedric, and they raced back and up the stairs to their room to change.

Half an hour later, after a swim in the warm Sea of Galilee, they stood together on a rock a few metres along from the hotel watching the fishermen casting their net. Jason glanced down at Cedric. Could it possibly be that he was going to stop being a pain?

☆ ☆ ☆

The next four days were unlike anything Jason had ever known. The two families had gone by coach through the valleys of Galilee, up 1200 feet into the city of Nazareth with its hundreds of whitewashed houses and narrow streets and bazaars, then down south along the valley of the River Jordan and into the ancient city of Jericho.

'*And the walls come a-tumblin' down*' sang Cedric as the chorus of voices joined in singing the old spiritual. Jason, even though it had been Cedric's idea, couldn't help joining in halfway through.

The public address system was switched on and the courier spoke. 'Now we are on our way to another very famous town, Bethlehem, where Jesus was born. From there we shall go to Jerusalem itself, where you will check in to your next hotel and be taken round the city, and then through the streets along the route which Jesus took from his trial to the place called Calvary, the scene of his Crucifixion, and then to where he was buried before his resurrection.'

Cedric held out a paper bag to Jason. 'Have a sweet?' 'Thanks,' said Jason. He examined it carefully for signs of poison before putting it in his mouth.

It was late afternoon when they arrived at the place where, according to tradition, Jesus had been buried. 'This is known as "The Garden Tomb",' said the courier. They were in a luxuriant garden, shady with trees and perfumed with the scent of flowers. They walked slowly toward what looked like a stone wall but was actually the face of a rock which had been cut vertically. At its centre a roughly round opening had been made, and this led into a dark interior. In front of the opening, cut into the rocky ground, was a narrow groove.

The courier spoke again, bending down and pointing to the groove. 'This is the track for the stone door—an enormous round disc which would be rolled along to cover the entrance to the tomb after the body had been buried. Think of the scene. Jesus had been buried all day Friday and Saturday. Now, it is just after sunrise on Sunday morning.' He opened a small pocket Bible and read from St John, chapter 20.

The Webbs, the Stevens and the rest of the group went inside the tomb one at a time and looked down at the stone floor.

Jason, as he stood on the very spot where the body of Jesus might have been laid, felt most peculiar. He felt quite unlike himself. He turned to his father who was standing in the narrow entrance. 'It's funny,' he said. He was whispering, yet his voice echoed round the walls. 'Suddenly it all seems real. I mean, he was really crucified, and he really died, and he really came alive again—he "rose again from the dead", like it says in the Creed we say in church on Sundays.'

The sun was setting as they came out of the tomb.

☆ ☆ ☆

Back in the city of Jerusalem they went into the hotel and got ready for the evening meal, after which one more expedition had been planned before bed: a night-time trip out into the hills to look back at the lights of the city.

After the meal Jason and Cedric stood on the hotel steps waiting for the others to assemble. The coach stood waiting by the kerb. The Jerusalem traffic hooted and rumbled past. Then a brightly-lit shop window next to the hotel caught Jason's eye.

'Five minutes to go—let's have a look in there while we're waiting,' he said.

They wandered along and stood looking in the window. The shop sold everything from model aircraft to transformers. 'Better than grey socks,' said Jason, and they went in. A big display of small gliders was by the door, and an assistant was throwing one of them. It sailed round in a circle and returned as though by magnetism to his hand. But not only that: it carried tiny flashing red lights in its nose, tail and wingtips. Again he threw it, and again it returned.

'Leviticus! That's brill!' breathed Jason.

'Yeah!' responded Cedric, looking at the pile of gliders, some blue, some red, waiting to be sold. Then he said, 'Hang on—Mum's got all my pocket money—I'm going to get it!' He raced from the shop, leaving Jason being observed suspiciously by the assistant.

'Your friend—he has taken a glider?'

'No, of course not! He's just gone to get some money —he's going to buy one.'

'I think he took one from the display,' said the assistant.

'No, he didn't! He's not a thief. He's all sorts of other things, but he's not a thief.'

A minute went by. Jason went to the door. 'Shall I just nip into the hotel and find him?' he said.

The man smiled a very worldly-wise smile and moved between Jason and the door.

'Oh, no,' he said. 'I'm afraid you must stay until he returns. You see, many people try this trick.'

'Trick? What trick?' said Jason.

The manager came out from a back office. 'You will wait here, please,' he said.

Jason came to a decision. The coach would be moving off any minute. He had to get into the hotel and get things sorted out. If he didn't hurry he would miss the coach. He acted so swiftly that he even surprised himself. As the manager turned to reach a telephone he made a dive for the door. It stuck. He wrenched at it and nearly fell as it jerked open. Once outside he ran like the wind, with the assistant after him.

But the coach was moving off.

Jason tore after it, catching up and banging on its side. How far he ran he couldn't tell, but as the coach cleared the traffic it accelerated and pulled away from him.

He looked behind him and saw the assistant ten metres away.

He turned and ran. A dark alley loomed up on his left and he shot into the darkness and hid in a dark doorway.

The assistant came slithering to a halt right opposite the doorway and saw Jason instantly.

'Come—with me,' he said.

☆ ☆ ☆

In the coach, Cedric turned to his mother. 'Crumbs!' he said.

'What, darling?'

'I've just thought! Jason's still in the shop! I forgot when you called me to get on the coach!'

'Jason? Shop? What shop?'

'What's that about Jason?' said Mrs Webb from her seat.

Mrs Stevens stood up and looked toward the back seats. 'Don't be silly, he's probably at the back with those other boys.' Mrs Webb wobbled up to them as the coach took a bend.

'Jason? Missing?' She stopped and turned to look for him. 'Cecilia, where's Jason?'

☆ ☆ ☆

Ten minutes later Jason, held firmly in his chair by the assistant, watched the shop door burst open. Cedric came in, followed by the Stevens, the Webbs, the courier, a policeman and a stray dog.

'Cedric—you rotten, stupid—' began Jason.

Cedric grinned sheepishly. 'Hi! Sorry. I got carried away.' Jason spluttered, Mr Stevens reassured the manager that nothing had been stolen, Mrs Stevens wagged her finger at Cedric, the Webbs looked at the courier and each other, the policeman started to say something important, and as the dog got bored and wandered out into the Jerusalem night Cedric said, 'I'd like one of the blue ones, please. Can I have my pocket money, Mum?'

Jason thought black thoughts in bed that night. But when he finally got to sleep he had a pleasant dream; he was making Cedric eat a special breakfast: six pairs of minced and boiled grey socks, without tomato sauce.

Jason and the Rogation Lark

The May morning sunshine of Rogation Sunday was tinted with the reds and blues of stained glass as it streamed down on to the choir of St Matthew's Church, Oakbridge.

The boys in the choir never actually looked forward to the vicar's talks, and yet once he had begun they would find themselves listening—he had a way of bringing the Bible to life, and you felt that if, as you went out through the west door, you found Elijah chatting to friends, or, down by the lych gate, Jesus healing a blind person, it would come as no great surprise. But something in the vicar's manner this morning made them all feel that this was going to be something particularly special.

'How many of you would be able to take a stranger round the village,' he began, 'and point out exactly where the village boundary is—all the way round?'

Jason dug his friend John in the ribs. 'Bet you I could,' he whispered. To his embarrassment the vicar turned in the pulpit and looked straight down at him and then back to the congregation.

'I understand,' he smiled, 'that someone not a million miles from where I'm standing thinks he could. Well, he doesn't know it, but he'll very soon have the chance to prove it! But first of all, let's look at Rogation Sunday; a lot of people think that it is just about "beating the bounds"—identifying boundaries. In fact, there is no real connection.

'The word "rogation", like most English words, comes from the Latin. "Rogare" is Latin for "to ask". And on Rogation Sunday, which always falls on the fifth Sunday after Easter, we ask for God's protection of our crops and for a good harvest.

'Why? Why should we do this on a particular day? Why should we ask for this particular thing on this particular day? The answer is a very common one in the Christian faith: because the Romans did! They had a ceremony called "Robigalia". They would go in procession round the cornfields—they probably did it here in Oakbridge—and they prayed to the Roman gods for preservation of the crops from mildew. After Christianity came to England, the Christians adopted the same kind of prayer, the same procession round the fields, and they did it at roughly the same time of year. But, of course, they prayed to God, and in the name of our Lord, Jesus Christ. It was linked to the greatest single event in the Christian year—Easter, and it was fixed at the fifth Sunday afterwards.

'Just now, we read in our second lesson . . .' he continued, and his voice floated out through the wide-open south door; out to the little churchyard where Oakbridge people had been buried for so many years that the inscriptions on some of the older gravestones were quite obliterated; out to one of the taller grave stones behind which leaned three men, smoking cigarettes. Now and then, a little high-pitched giggle was smothered behind a hand. On close inspection one would have seen that they were hardly men at all—the oldest was no more than fifteen.

'Well, come on!' said one. 'If I'm going to join in this lark of yours I want to know what you've got going. All I know is the old vicar's going to lead his little gang round the fields and say stupid prayers and stuff—right?'

'Right,' one of them said in a whisper, 'and we've taken the cover off of that old drain by the pylon, and we done up the hole real good so's it's got grass an' mud an' stuff all over it—an' it's right on the footpath, see, so they'll come trippin' along—' but all three were doubled up with giggles, snorts and other signs of hysterical agony.

The noise reached through the open south door and echoed up the aisle.

☆ ☆ ☆

Sunday lunch in Jason's home was always a happy affair. There was usually someone invited, and today their neighbours, the Davis's—together with Old Man Davis—were there, and the St Matthew's choirmaster, Adrian Jackson.

Mrs Webb smiled at him over the roast lamb. 'Well, Adrian, all ready for the wedding? It's only a fortnight away!' She laughed. 'Fancy, our choirmaster getting married! Seems only yesterday you were telling us all you would be a bachelor for the rest of your life!'

Mr Jackson smiled. 'We get wiser as we get older! Yes, it's all coming together gradually. The choir's doing a great job with the music for the service, and a friend of mine's coming to play the organ.'

'Talking of services,' said Old Man Davis, 'can anyone tell me exactly what we're supposed to do this afternoon on the Rogation procession?'

His son looked up. 'Yes—I was wondering, too. I reckon that's a jolly good idea of the vicar's,' he said. 'Come on, Adrian, tell us all about it.'

'Well, what happens is that we meet at the church at three o'clock, sing a hymn, then we go in procession down the lane, up the footpath by the post box and along the edge of Copley Woods. Then we go left by the pylon and follow the path right round till we come to the lane, then back up to the church. Then there's tea in the church hall.'

Cecilia broke in. 'And, horror of horrors, Cedric Stevens is taking a photograph of the procession half-way round, and I've got to be with him. Although just why it has to be me, I've no idea, Mr Jackson!'

'I think you're one of the few people who can keep Cedric on a short leash!' he said. 'And I'm most grateful. He pleaded with me to let him do it—he hasn't got a camera of his own so he's borrowing his father's. I understand from a professional-photographer friend of mine that Cedric has quite a natural talent for photography.'

'And I gather we're "beating the bounds" on the way,' said Old Man Davis. 'We haven't done that in Oakbridge since I was a boy. We used to do it every year when I was a chorister in St Matthew's.'

'Yes,' said Jason, 'and you know what? We've got to be whacked on the bum with willow branches!'

Mrs Webb coughed loudly. 'Jason! Please!—Yes, Mr Davis, I've never really understood that. What was the point of that—hitting poor little boys on their backsides when they hadn't done anything wrong!'

Mr Davis laughed. 'I don't think they did it with any force or malice. It was just a way of teaching the boys, who would one day become the tenants and farmers, exactly where the boundary of the village was—north, south, east and west. I mean, there were no such things as local maps, then. So they reckoned that a bit of a whack on the whatsit was the best way of making them remember.'

'But I thought they hit the soil, as well as the boys, with the willow branches,' said the choirmaster.

'Yes—but that was an alternative—the whole thing was done differently in different parts of the country.'

Mrs Webb started collecting the empty plates. 'And does it have anything to do with Rogation Sunday?'

'Oh, absolutely nothing! It happened something like this. In 1559 the whole Rogation idea was stopped. Then, when Elizabeth the First came to the throne, she brought it back again, the processions and everything. Beating the bounds became a part of the Rogation procession—I suppose she decided that if you're going to process round the village anyway, you might just as well teach the boys the boundaries at the same time!'

Jason was about to ask if anyone had discovered what all the laughing in the churchyard had been about, when his mother placed on the table the kind of pudding that makes conversation impossible.

☆ ☆ ☆

'Now, would you all please listen for a moment!' It was a quarter-to-three, and in the church the vicar was up on the chancel steps. 'Just a few words about this procession. First of all, the reason. We're doing it primarily as a little act of witness to the community, to show that we believe God is our creator and the creator of everything round us. Then, we are reminding ourselves of our heritage—of the hundreds of men and women before us who helped to make this village, and who trusted in the very same God for the crops.

'Now, would you form up in the following order . . .' At precisely three o'clock, Mr Jackson played over the first verse of a hymn and they all sang lustily. At the end, the choirboys and choirmen, followed by the congregation of about thirty men, women and children wound their way up the lane, round past the postbox, and up by Copley Woods.

☆ ☆ ☆

Cedric, with Jason's sister Cecilia keeping a careful eye on him, crouched by the path and squinted through the viewfinder of his father's camera.

'I think we should move along a bit,' he said. 'Look—you see that bit of grass and mud and stuff all over the path? If I go there I shall be able to see all the procession as it turns up past the postbox, then the woods will be in the background, nice and dark.' He got up and went toward the litter of grass, twigs and soil, stopping short by a meter or so. He squatted down again and peered through the lens. He was unaware of a movement in the bushes beside him.

The last small girl in the procession had just passed the postbox and turned up toward Copley Woods when the vicar turned, held up his hand, and called, 'Friends, this is our first stop. We are now right on the northernmost boundary of Oakbridge. This would have been the spot where, for hundreds of years, until about fifty years ago, the boys of the village would have been taught a little lesson!' There was a ripple of laughter down the procession. 'Jason and John are the first two boys to represent the lads of the village—step this way, please!'

Both secretly wishing they had never agreed to do this, they stepped forward, cassocks and surplices blowing in the breeze, and, going to where the vicar was standing with a bundle of willow twigs, bent over. A photographer from the local paper came forward, and as the willows lightly descended on alternate posteriors, the flashgun fired and preserved the moment for the newspapers on village breakfast tables the following Tuesday.

'Not too painful, chaps?' smiled the vicar. Mr Webb overheard the question and called out, 'You can be a bit rougher next time, vicar—it'll make up for lost time!'

'Let's go and grab 'im now . . .'

The procession moved on.

☆ ☆ ☆

In the bushes by the pylon the three youths watched Cedric creeping closer to the booby-trapped drain and held their breath.

'Stupid kid—he'll fall in himself if he goes any closer! Let's go and grab 'im now before that lot comes round —he'll spoil everything,' said one of them.

Cedric, happily unaware of any of the plans being made for him, composed the picture in his viewfinder. It was good—except—perhaps, just a little closer? He moved forward.

At that moment the vicar turned the corner. From his point of view, what happened next was all most peculiar, *most* peculiar. Yes, he thought, Cedric was there all ready with his camera, moving forward a few paces. But why were three young men rushing out from the bushes? And how could it be that these three very solid-looking young men were at one moment in mid-flight toward Cedric and the next—nowhere? How could they simply vanish?

The vicar ran forward, followed by choir and congregation. Cedric stood by the gaping hole in the ground, fascinated, as three very wet, muddy humans tried quite unsuccessfully to scramble out of the pit.

'Cedric, what on earth is going on?' said the vicar.

'Sir, they jumped out at me just as I was going to get in a better position for the picture, and I jumped out of the way, and they jumped into the pit—but there wasn't a pit there before—'

'It was a trap,' said Cecilia. 'All covered up with grass and sticks—look, the real cover is over by those bushes!'

'And I would guess,' said Constable Jeffries, who was one of the basses in the choir, 'that the trap was meant for you, vicar, not to mention the boys following. Now, come on, out of it!' he said to the three young men in the pit, and reached down to help them out one by one. He looked up and grinned. 'Quite a bumper crop, vicar!'

Five minutes later, the three youths were shambling along beside the constable toward the police station, the wet denim and billowing white surplice making an odd contrast.

And the rest of the choir and congregation went on their way, to beat the bounds and to ask God's blessing on the crops.

As for the vicar, he was making a mental note to pay a friendly visit to the three young men and, much to his own surprise, asking God's blessing on Cedric Stevens.

Jason and the Whitsun Dream

Jason, in his jazzy blue swimming trunks, lay flat on his back on the lawn in the back garden. Eyes shut, he felt the sun burning some colour into his winter-white skin. He wiggled his toes to the beat of a tune in his head.

It was Whit Sunday. His parents and sister had gone to visit an elderly relative and he had been charged with looking after the house for the afternoon.

'Now, we don't want a crowd of your friends round here making a commotion and disturbing the neighbours, mind,' Mrs Webb had said, tapping the tip of his nose in the way that told him that, whilst she meant every word she said, she was trying not to be severe.

Well, he thought, sighing comfortably and shifting his head to a more comfortable position, all his friends were busy, anyway. And as for making a racket it was the last thing he wanted. Just a bit of peace and quiet. He might even drop off to sleep.

An observer would have seen a bird land beside him, not noticing him. Jason sneezed. The bird left with a tremendous squawk of fright and a whirring of wings. Jason opened one eye, and shut it again. The afternoon droned quietly on, a lawnmower humming a long way away, a small child chattering happily somewhere, and a bird twittering nervously in the oak tree down the garden.

The same observer would have noticed Jason's chest moving up and down more and more regularly and his toes ceasing to wiggle.

Jason was not aware of these signs, however. He was more concerned about a noise. A commotion, his mother would have called it. It sounded like a crowd of people a long way away but making a real racket.

The noise came gradually nearer. He could pick out his friend John's voice, then Spud's and Henry's. Mrs Jones the postmistress was shouting something excitedly, the vicar was calling out to Mr Jackson the choirmaster and Old Man Davis was trying to make Cedric Stevens hear what he wanted to say.

They were all round him, now, and more people were flooding in through the side gate and spilling out all over the lawn and the flowerbeds and the vegetable garden. 'Leviticus!' thought Jason, 'Mum'll go stark staring mad—and as for Dad . . .' the thought made him shudder.

The really odd thing about it all was that there were so many total strangers. There were Chinese and Japanese; there were people from all over the African continent; from India and Pakistan, from Russia and Iceland and Jamaica—Jason was quite sure where they came from, but he could not have explained how he knew. He just knew.

The garden was crammed to capacity, now. Jason had a good view of them all—he was in his favourite spot up the old apple tree. He spotted Old Man Davis worming his way through the crowd toward the steps that led from the lawn up to the house.

It was then that the oddest thing of all happened. As Old Man Davis went up the steps, it became dark. There seemed to be a roof overhead. Jason looked up, and found he was not in the garden after all, but in the Assembly Hall at school. He was not in the apple tree but sitting in one of the ancient high windows, on the window sill, his legs dangling over the people's heads.

And Mr Davis was not going up the steps to the house, but up the carpeted steps to the platform, and now he was standing at the reading desk.

Mr Davis clapped his hands for silence, but the noise was staggering. Everyone was talking in his own language and no one seemed to be able to understand what anyone else was talking about. Slowly, people began to notice that someone was trying to address them from the platform.

'Ladies and Gentlemen, it is good to welcome you all here today on this very special occasion.' Old Man Davis smiled round at the now silent gathering.

'As you all know, today is Pentecost, and we are gathered here to thank God for his gifts at Harvest time.'

'Harvest time?' thought Jason. 'In May?' Ah, well. So many funny things were going on that anything was possible.

'Now, there are many strangers and visitors here in Jerusalem with us today,' went on Old Man Davis, 'so for their benefit I shall explain briefly why we Jews are here today and what it is that we are doing—' ('Jews?' thought Jason. 'Jerusalem?' Then he sighed and settled down to listen)—'and I'm sure those Jerusalem residents who are able to speak a few languages will be pleased to interpret for me in a moment or two.

'Seven weeks and one day ago, we Jewish people celebrated the festival of Passover, remembering when God passed over the Israelites' houses when he punished the Egyptians by killing all the firstborn of Egypt. Then came the festival of Firstfruits, when we offered God our very first fruits of the Harvest. Today, it is the end of the grain harvest, and our priest will offer two loaves of bread made from the newly-ground flour, along with animal sacrifices.'

There was a brief buzz of conversation as some of the residents who could speak various foreign languages interpreted Old Man Davis's words for the benefit of nearby visitors. Jason saw Cedric with a group of very large and affectionate French ladies—he was struggling in first-year French to explain the meaning of Passover, and as he flung his arms up into the air to demonstrate the passage of the angels of death one of the larger ladies was quite overcome with affection and grasped him by the waist, hugged him to her and planted a wet kiss on his cheek. Jason was delighted to see Cedric go bright crimson, and then he had one of his brilliant ideas.

'But now,' continued Old Man Davis, when the hubbub had dropped, 'we are at the Festival of Pentecost—which is simply Greek for "fifty days", it being fifty days since Passover—and we shall be celebrating with a great deal of singing and dancing and generally enjoying ourselves. Needless to say, you will all be most welcome to join in our festivities.'

The moment Old Man Davis finished speaking a band struck up a lively melody from somewhere in the hall, and people began to dance. A big circle was formed, the men and women and children all involved in a complicated set of movements.

Jason didn't remember actually jumping down from his perch on the windowsill, but he found himself joining in.

☆ ☆ ☆

Meanwhile, Cedric, far from being asleep and dreaming, was wide awake and enjoying himself tremendously. He had been going up and down the street on his skateboard for about half an hour on this hot, Whit Sunday afternoon, when he spotted Jaws, the Davis's cat, wandering in through Jason Webb's front garden gate.

'Jaws' was not the Davis's name for their cat. Their name for him was Tibbles. 'Jaws' was Cedric's own name for him since he had been nipped on his left forefinger while teasing the old tabby cat with a stick. To have another go at teasing Jaws seemed to Cedric to be the perfect way to spend the rest of the hot afternoon, and he followed the cat up the Webb's front path. He fished about in the pocket of his shorts and found a length of string. He picked up a small twig and tied it to the end of the string.

He made squeaking noises with his lips and Jaws stopped and turned round. Cedric trailed the twig along the path. Jaws crouched, waggled his hind quarters, and pounced. Cedric snatched the string and the twig, and Jaws sat down and washed his face. Unable to face Cedric and defeat, he then turned and jumped up on to the side gate and disappeared down the other side. Cedric paused. Should he follow him? Well, why not.

He unlatched the gate and went in. Jaws was stalking purposefully away toward the lawn and a patch of shade under the apple tree.

Cedric stopped, and looked. There, on the far edge of the lawn, flat on his back and apparently fast asleep, was Jason.

Jason, asleep. Jason, unaware. Jason, vulnerable. Cedric's face twisted into the mixture of terrible pain and enormous happiness that meant trouble for Jason.

☆ ☆ ☆

The dancing and singing was reaching a crescendo in the Assembly Hall. Jason was getting out of breath with the action and the excitement and he was quite relieved when the music came to a stop. He flopped down on to a wooden form that ran down one side of the hall. An African boy came and sat with him.

But in place of the music was a strange sound. The nearest Jason could get to identifying the sound was that it was a bit like a very high wind whistling round the windows and doors of the school building. But there was no wind—the windows were wide open and the long curtains hung straight and still. The noise became louder and louder. The crowd began to be afraid, and Old Man Davis jumped up on to the platform again.

'Ladies and Gentlemen,' he called out, 'don't worry! It's perfectly all right! There's probably one of those street cleaning trucks outside—they make that extraordinary noise!'

The band started again, competing with the strange noise.

Jason and the African boy were watching as the dancing re-started when a shout from Old Man Davis stopped everything.

'Look! Look!' he called, and his voice was no longer quiet and comforting. He sounded alarmed, and the sense of fear spread quickly through the crowd. People drew together in little groups, children clung to parents' hands.

Jason looked to where Old Man Davis was pointing. He could hardly believe his own eyes. The Headmaster, standing with a group of people over by the main door, had a flame coming out of the top of his head.

People gasped and clutched at each other as they looked. Then, one by one, more flames appeared, each one resting on top of someone's head. Soon, every head in the hall had a flame hovering and flickering above it, until the crowd of people looked for all the world like a cluster of candles. The sound of the wind continued, yet there was no wind and each flame burned straight upwards and not bending to any wind.

Jason saw an enormous man falling towards him.

Now a further crowd was gathering outside and pushing its way into the already crowded hall. Near panic broke out as the newcomers saw what was happening.

Jason was dismayed and terrified. Then the final extraordinary thing happened. The Oakbridge people were all talking to the foreign strangers—the Russians, Greeks, Italians and so on—and they were talking in the language of the foreigners! Jason started to speak to the boy next to him, and found himself speaking in fluent Swahili.

Now the newcomers were laughing and pointing at the Oakbridge people. 'Why, they're all dead drunk!' they were shouting. 'Look at them, gabbling away in gibberish!'

Old Man Davis heard what they were saying, and held up his hand. The sound of the wind had stopped now, and the flames had vanished.

'Ladies and Gentlemen,' he said quietly, and there was a hush. 'These people are not drunk, as you have suggested. They have been filled with the Holy Spirit of God! Don't you remember what the prophet Joel said all those years ago? He said that God would pour out his Spirit on all people . . . and this is what is happening now!'

There was a great surge of movement in the huge crowd of people, and Jason saw an enormous man falling towards him. He landed heavily on Jason's lap and Jason was struggling to push him off when he heard a familiar sound.

It was Cedric's voice, and Cedric was laughing.

Jason opened his eyes, and sat up. He was in his swimming trunks, and he was on the back lawn. Jaws, the Davis's cat, was streaking away across the lawn with his tail in the air, Cedric was standing there with a stick on a piece of string, laughing so much that he couldn't stand up straight, and Old Man Davis was walking towards them from the side passage.

'Hullo—there he is!' he laughed. 'Been hunting for Tibbles everywhere! Why, Jason, you look bewildered! What's happened?'

Cedric answered the question as he started walking quickly toward the side gate. 'Oh,' he said, casually, 'Jaws—I mean Tibbles—accidentally jumped straight on to Jason's chest while he was asleep—'bye everyone!' But Jason saw the twig and the string and knew instantly what had actually happened.

He stood up, rubbing his eyes, and Old Man Davis picked up the cat. 'I just had the most fantastic dream,' said Jason. 'You remember the sermon we had in church this morning—about Whitsun and the coming of the Holy Spirit and Peter and the Apostles and all the crowd at Pentecost and the sound of wind that wasn't there and the flames on the Apostles' heads and—and—'

'You dreamed you were there?' said the man.

'Yes,—it was so real—exactly like the vicar said it was.'

'Was I there?' smiled Old Man Davis.

'Oh, yes—you were Peter!'

'What about Cedric? Was he there?'

'Certainly was!' Jason thought a moment. Then he said, 'Mr Davis, by the way, you don't know any very large ladies who like kissing little boys, do you?'

It was Mr Davis's turn to look bewildered.

Jason and the Trinity Trip

Jason was doing 115 mph over Oakbridge and enjoying himself—actually enjoying himself, he thought, without Cedric spoiling everything. He pinched his leg to make sure it was not a dream. Sure enough, it hurt.

Twenty-four hours ago he had been in the middle of the R.E. period learning about The Holy Trinity. If someone had whispered that tomorrow would find him whistling over the steeple of St Matthew's Church in a sleek black-and-red Piper 'Warrior' he would probably have said, 'Pull the other leg—it's got bells on!' and carried on listening to the R.E. teacher grappling with the mystery of the Trinity. But nobody did whisper and all he could hear was the R.E. teacher's voice.

'God is three persons, yet those three persons are one. Webb, can you tell us the names of the three persons of the Holy Trinity?'

'God the Father, God the Son, and God the Holy Spirit,' said Jason.

'Right. Now, you've all seen a hologram—a three-dimensional image made by shining a laser beam through a special glass plate. If I were to take that plate and smash it into three pieces and then shine the beam through one of those pieces, what would the image look like? Yes, Cater?'

Jason's friend Spud looked dubious as he said, 'Would it be one-third of the image, Sir?'

'Afraid not! And that's the crazy thing about holographic plates—we would still see the whole image; a bit dimmer than with a full plate, but still complete. Even if the plates were smashed into a thousand pieces, one fragment would still produce a whole image.

'And the holographic plate is a good illustration of the Trinity. Each member of the Holy Trinity is equal to the other two members and each is able to do the work of all three. Now, homework! I want you to try to think of another good illustration of the Trinity and be ready to tell us about it the day after tomorrow, Second Period.'

As he spoke, the door opened and the Head came in. He spoke to the R.E. teacher, who nodded and looked at Jason.

'Webb—would you go with the Head to his office for a few minutes, please.'

☆ ☆ ☆

Jason, Spud, Henry and John were unlocking their bikes after school. 'What did he want?' said Spud.

'Yes—come on, tell us!' said the other two to Jason, weaving their way across the playground to the lane.

'It's my uncle from Tasmania. He's a pilot with a charter airline and they've sent him over to England to start up another company here—well, at Oakchester Flying Club. Little aircraft, like Pipers and Cessnas.'

'What's that got to do with you, though?' said Henry, coming up from the rear and overtaking Jason.

'He rang Dad to say he was coming tomorrow and wanted to know if I could spend a day with him at the airfield—he hasn't seen me since I was born. My sister's at boarding school so he can't see her—he's only here for a day. Dad rang the school, and told the Head, and the Head said I could have tomorrow off school.'

'Lucky thing!' said John, Henry and Spud together. Then John called out from behind, 'Hey, what about choir practice tomorrow night?'

'Don't worry—I'll be there! You got any ideas for R.E. homework? The Trinity thing? I haven't got a clue what to do. I mean, what else is three in one and one in three?'

'Search me,' said Spud, doing wheelies.

'You must be joking,' said John, also doing wheelies.

Henry was about to say something of the same sort but found himself lying in a ditch with his bike on top of him. Henry was not very good at wheelies.

☆ ☆ ☆

A red Mercedes stood purring quietly outside the Webb's house at seven the next morning, with Jason's Uncle Charles waiting patiently at the wheel. Eventually, Jason came shooting out of the front door struggling into his coat and trying to wipe toothpaste off his chin. The phone in the front hall started ringing as he clambered into the passenger seat and his mother was waving the phone at him and calling out as the heavy, leather-lined door slammed and Jason, without a backward glance, was whisked smoothly away down the village street and out into the country.

'My company wants to start a charter business in small, light aircraft—two seaters and four-seaters,' said Charles Webb. 'That sort of thing. They want to open up here in England, and we've fixed it all up with Oakchester Flying Club. I'm going to have a meeting with the Directors today—shouldn't take long—then I'm going to take one of their new Piper "Warrior" kites up for a trial flight.'

☆ ☆ ☆

Jason lay on the grass watching the daily business of running a flying club. Uncle Charles was still in the meeting with the Directors. A blue Piper Cub landed with a series of bounces, opened up and took off again with a growl.

He fished in his pocket and pulled out the Mars Bar his mother had given him. He frowned. Even though he wasn't doing lessons at school, even though it was a beautiful day, and in spite of his uncle's promise to take him up in the 'Warrior', he was worried.

Normally, when Jason was worried it was Cedric Stevens who was the reason. But today Cedric couldn't possibly spoil things. Today, the only cloud on Jason's horizon was that wretched business of homework for tomorrow. The R.E. teacher was particularly fond of making them stand up and give their homework answers in front of the form instead of writing them down. He also specialised in making you feel uncomfortable if you hadn't got it right.

He frowned harder still to see if it would bring an idea. 'Three in one and one in three,' he muttered, twisting the hair at the crown of his head until it looked more like an aerial.

'Sorry? What was that?' said his uncle's voice from just behind him. Jason jumped up and flushed bright red.

'Nothing—just, er, practising homework.'

'Right. All set? Let's go, then.' They went quickly over to where a brand new Piper 'Warrior' stood waiting for them outside the flying school hangar. All thoughts of homework, together with the frown, vanished.

☆ ☆ ☆

Mrs Webb had shut the front door and spoken into the phone as the Mercedes swept away down the road. 'Sorry, Cedric, but you've just missed Jason. Can I help?'

'Well, no, thanks all the same,' said the small voice at the other end. 'Only, I've been given an ace present and it's a flying model aircraft and it's not even my birthday and I wondered if Jason could help me with it but it's all right 'cos Spud knows about these and I'll ask him.'

'Well, that's all right, then,' said Mrs Webb.

☆ ☆ ☆

At ten thousand feet the little red Piper aircraft levelled off and began a slow turn to starboard.

Jason watched the duplicate set of controls in front of him move as his uncle manouevred the aircraft with his own. There was a half wheel, like half of a car's steering wheel, and two pedals that came out of the floor by his feet.

Charles Webb turned to him. 'An aircraft is basically a tube with two sets of wings—big ones halfway down the tube and small ones at the back. The small ones have an upright wing, called the fin, standing between them. There's a moveable bit on the back edge of all three, and that's the bit that makes the aircraft change direction—left, right, up and down.

'The moveable bits on the two main wings are called ailerons. When one of them moves up, the opposite one moves down—that makes the aircraft tip onto its side, ready for turning. The small wings at the back—the tail-plane—have similar moveable bits but they both move in the same direction. When they tip upwards the tail is pushed down and so the aircraft goes up. They're called the elevators.

'The fin's moveable bit is called the rudder—which works exactly like the rudder on a boat, so there's no need to say more about that.

'Now, watch.' Charles Webb, with the control wheel held loosely in both hands, turned it to the right and pulled back a little. The plane tipped to the right but carried on in the same direction. Then he pressed the right-hand pedal, and the plane began going to the right in a slow, banking turn. He straightened out and said, 'Still watching?'

Jason nodded energetically. This was infinitely better than school. His uncle opened the throttle slightly and pulled back on the wheel. The control column emerged slowly from the instrument panel. The horizon dropped out of sight below the windscreen as the aircraft climbed upwards.

After a few more simple manoeuvres, he said to Jason, 'I've had your seat specially adjusted so that you can reach the controls—so, now she's all yours.'

Jason stared at him. 'Leviticus!' he gulped, then gripped the wheel and stamped quickly on to the two pedals.

'First lesson—don't grip the wheel and just rest your feet lightly.' Pale-faced and pop-eyed, Jason nodded.

The smart new plane wobbled about the sky as Jason tried to co-ordinate hands and feet. But within a few minutes the wings were remaining level and the tail had stopped waggling round and round.

'There's Oakbridge, straight ahead.'

Jason gave a yelp of delight. 'Look! There's St Matthew's Church!' The aircraft was now wobbling considerably more than it had been and Charles took a firmer grip on the controls.

'Hang on,' he said, 'I'll go round in a wide turn and we'll shoot them up a bit.' They turned to port and swung in a

St Matthew's steeple stood out clearly as they came closer and closer.

wide arc round the countryside, crossing the River Ock as it flowed out of the city of Oakchester, passing the cathedral and the city outskirts. They did the full circle and Charles pushed the wheel forward slightly. Jason watched the horizon climb up the windscreen and saw Oakbridge in the distance. St Matthew's steeple stood out clearly as they came closer and closer, growing bigger every second. The fields were no longer just green patches; they had real hedges and real cows were grazing there. The sun glinted on a car as it went along the lane below them, and suddenly they were roaring low over Jason's house. Then Jason let out another shout. In the lane, outside the row of cottages next to the general stores and newspaper shop, he had quite clearly seen two boys kneeling on the narrow pavement, examining something. It had been a fleeting glimpse, but the two were unmistakeable. They were Spud and Cedric.

☆ ☆ ☆

'Oh,' said Jason casually in response to Spud's enquiry the next morning in the playground before school, 'quite good'. He was about to mention his sighting of Spud and Cedric in the High Street but decided he would leave that till later.

'Bet you didn't actually fly it, though.'

'How much?'

'You mean you did?'

'Of course. As a matter of fact if you don't believe me here's a certificate to prove it—' Jason pulled an envelope from his pocket and took out a small sheet of headed notepaper. 'There! Read that!'

THIS IS TO CERTIFY THAT JASON WEBB, OF WEBB'S FARM, OAKBRIDGE, TODAY FLEW A PIPER 'WARRIOR' FOR FIVE MINUTES AT THE PUPIL'S CONTROLS.

The note was signed 'Charles Webb, Director'.

'And he took a picture of me in the cockpit,' said Jason, who was beginning to feel very superior to Spud. At that moment the rest of the gang came running up to him.

'Jason—what happened?'

'Did you get a trip in the plane?'

'Was it good?'

Jason felt more and more important. He felt like a god among all these boys. They seemed so simple, so inexperienced. He examined his fingernails without saying anything for a moment, then he said, 'Well, actually, it was all a bit of a bore—I already knew quite a bit about aircraft and flying and stuff, port and starboard and all that. Still, it was a day off school, so I s'pose it was all right,' and he pushed past them and sauntered toward the school door.

He had just reached the doorway when he felt his heart do a somersault in his chest. The homework! He'd forgotten all about the homework! In a state of sheer panic he turned and ran toward the shrubbery and the school garden. There, out of sight, he stopped. What could he say to the R.E. teacher? Three in one and one in three . . . He hadn't a clue what to say. Terrified, he went back into the lobby just as the bell sounded.

First period was over far too quickly, and now the R.E. teacher was standing in front of them.

'Right! Homework on the Holy Trinity,' he said, rubbing his hands with anticipation of some good illustrations. 'Let's have you first, Cater. Come out to the front, please.'

Spud made his way out from the desks and faced the form.

'Well,' he said, 'I think I've got as close to it as possible. You see, I think the Holy Trinity is a bit like an aircraft.'

Jason came out of his big black cloud with a rush. Spud! What did *he* know about aircraft? Nothing!

But the very thought of an aircraft did something inside Jason's brain which gave him the very answer he had been searching for. Of course—three controls for one plane! Elevators, ailerons and rudder! Three controls, one plane! Three in one! Now he could beat them all!

Spud was warming up. 'And, you see,' he said, waving his arms as though drawing an aeroplane in space, 'you've got three controls and one aircraft—the elevators, the ailerons and the rudder.'

Jason gulped, disbelieving.

'Three controls but only one plane,' Spud went on. 'Of course, my illustration isn't perfect because the elevators can't do the job of the other two, and so on, but . . .'

'Excellent, excellent!' said the R.E. teacher, rubbing his hands even harder. 'But how is it that you know so much about aircraft controls, Cater?'

'Oh, well, um—' Spud seemed suddenly bashful in front of the form. 'Well, actually it was a first-form boy yesterday lunchtime—he asked me to help put together a radio-controlled model aircraft, and I thought of the illustration while I was working the joystick on the control box.'

'Most resourceful of you, Cater. Just as a matter of interest, which particular first-former was it?'

The answer came from another desk, another voice; a very subdued, miserable voice.

'Cedric Stevens,' groaned Jason.

Jason and the Mystery Apostle

It was the Friday before Sunday, June 11, and the St Matthew's Church Choir Vestry rocked to the sound of a full choir singing lustily. Jason Webb, who was in line for promotion to Head Choirboy before long, was singing his loudest. Cedric Stevens, the smallest, who was not in line for anything—although he had lately been trying very hard—was singing loudly and very nearly in tune.

One boy was a stranger. Mr Jackson had introduced him as 'Peter', who was visiting Oakbridge for the weekend and was going to sing with the choir for both services on Sunday.

'Now Peter Jenkinson,' said the choirmaster, 'has got a very interesting second Christian name.'

There were various whispered suggestions and giggles which stopped when their visitor, Peter, who was easily the biggest boy there, looked round with a very fierce expression.

'And I've had an idea,' went on the choirmaster. 'You see, Peter's second name is in the Bible. What I want you to do between now and Sunday morning is to find out what it is—*but you must not ask him himself.* I'm going to give you a few clues, and then the first boy to come to me with the correct name will get a small prize—a Mars Bar, in fact. But now, let's get on with the practice!'

When the practice came to an end everyone prompted Mr Jackson to give them a clue.

'I'm going to give you two,' he said. 'The first one is this. This Bible character's name—and Peter's second name—ends—*ends*, mind you—with the letter "s". That's clue number one. Clue number two is this: he was a close friend of someone even more famous than himself. And I'll tell you just one more fact—you'll find him in the Acts of the Apostles. Now, on Sunday morning there will be a final clue on the notice board.'

After practice, one of the basses went up to Mr Jackson, smiling. 'Tell me, did this chap have anything to do with Cyprus?' he said.

'Most certainly he did!' replied the choirmaster.

'In that case,' said the bass—who was Constable Jeffries of the Oakbridge Police Station, 'we must be talking about—'

Mr Jackson held up his hand and looked round at the still-open door. 'Ssh! Walls have ears, Constable!'

☆ ☆ ☆

Hugo Smart was not the most popular member of the choir. He had an unfortunate way of telling unpleasant tales about other people—tales that usually were only partly true.

He also had a name for cheating whenever there was any kind of race or competition at school or choir.

But Peter, the weekend visitor, was not to know this, and when he found Hugo cycling along beside him on his way back to his aunt's house, where he was staying, he simply smiled in a friendly way and said, 'Hi!'

'Er—hullo,' smiled Hugo. 'You going my way?'

They pedalled along together, chatting. 'Staying here long?' asked Hugo, beginning to breathe heavily—Peter was much fitter and a good deal more muscular.

'Just for the weekend—going home on Sunday night.'

'I see you're a member,' puffed Hugo, 'of the World Wildlife Fund—I like wild animals and things, too.'

'That's great. Are you a member, too?'

'No, I'm not, actually—but I'd like to be. And it'd be good to have a friend I could write to about, well, foxes and hares and pheasants and stuff—could I write to you?'

'Why not! Got my address?'

'Er. no But if you hang on a bit I'll write it in my notebook.' Hugo wobbled to a halt and jammed a foot into the grassy bank. He fished about in his jacket and found his notebook and a stub of pencil. Peter had stopped just ahead of him and was turning to watch these preparations. A knowing smile was spreading over his face.

'Right,' said Hugo. 'Let's see, it's Peter, isn't it? Peter what?'

'Peter Jenkinson,' said the other boy, still smiling.

'Address?'

Peter dictated it slowly.

'Right,' said Hugo. Then he hesitated. 'Er—so that's just P. Jenkinson, is it? Isn't there a second initial? Only, I like to get all the details in my address book, see. And then I can put your full initials on the envelope, too.'

'Oh, yes—it's D,' smiled Peter. 'Now, shall we go?'

'That's D for—what?' said Hugo as casually as he could.

Peter tried to keep from laughing. With a serious frown to help him he replied, 'Oh, er, Dennis. Now, ready to go home?'

Hugo smirked at his cleverness and obvious success. 'Ah—er—no, I've just remembered I've left something behind,' he said, stuffing his notebook back into his jacket pocket. And, smiling smugly, he turned his bike round.

☆ ☆ ☆

Unknown to either Hugo or Peter Jenkinson, they had been followed at some distance by Cedric. Cedric was watching them carefully as they chatted and stood on their pedals navigating the up-and-down journey back to Oakbridge village.

He talked to himself. 'Now,' he said, leaning forward over the handlebars and streamlining himself in the light headwind, 'I wouldn't mind betting Hugo's getting that chap Peter to tell him what his second name is. Oh, well, two can play at that game! Only some of us,' he puffed as he topped the hill behind them and saw Peter moving off and Hugo putting his notebook into his pocket, 'some of us are better at it than others—and some of us need the right answer more than others, too.'

Then he called out, 'Oy! Hugo! Hang on a bit! Any idea what this chap's second name is, then?'

'Oh, yes—it's easy,' said Hugo, standing astride his crossbar. 'I know the Acts of the Apostles well—it's the name of a very well-known character.'

Hugo thought quickly of some other name he could fob Cedric off with. He hoisted himself on to the saddle and tried to balance with both feet off the ground and did not succeed.

Cedric cleared his throat. 'Look, Hugo, you know the prize is a Mars Bar—well if you tell me what the name is, I'll go and tell Mr Jackson and then he'll give me the Mars Bar but I'll give it straight to you. Promise! Only, you see, well, I want to get my light blue ribbon quickly and if I win this prize he might think about giving me my ribbon a bit sooner.'

'Er, well—you promise to let me have the Mars Bar?'

'Yes—of course!'

'All right, then.' Hugo had thought of a good name. He bent over and whispered in Cedric's ear. 'It's Theophilus,' he said. Cedric let out a whoop, shouted 'Thanks a lot!' and shot away over the brow of the hill towards home.

Hugo smirked. 'That'll teach the little squirt to try being clever!' he breathed. 'Anyway, any idiot knows it's Dennis.'

☆ ☆ ☆

Jason was in a hurry. He pushed his bike up their side passage, opened the back door and yelled 'Hi, Mum!' Then he went to the shed and brought his newly-painted skateboard out on to the pavement, stepped carefully on to the dazzling colours and whizzed away down the gentle hill toward the Davis's farm.

Ten minutes later he was sitting comfortably on the settee in a book-lined study with one hand clutching an orange Slushpuppy—of which Old Man Davis kept a stock in his fridge ready for the onslaught of grandchildren, neighbours

He was sitting comfortably . . . clutching an orange Slushpuppy.

and friends—and the other scratching between the ears of Tibbles, a large and very silky-furred black cat. Old Man Davis was referring to a leather-bound book.

'Now, I'm pretty sure I know what this name is,' he said, 'and as you say I'm not allowed to tell you what it is I'll try to tell you something about the character himself. Well, he went on a very long journey with a man called—'

'Ah—you mustn't tell me his name, either!' said Jason.

'How very honest of you! Right. Well, he went on a long journey—a missionary journey—with this other very famous character. He was described by the person who wrote The Acts of The Apostles as "a good man, full of the Holy Spirit and of faith". He was a Jew, and he came from Cyprus—so he was called a Cypriot Jew.'

'I think I know now who the very famous person was —and we're allowed to guess,' said Jason. 'I think it was St Paul.'

'Correct! Well, now, that makes it easier for me to tell you about B—' he clapped a hand to his mouth—'I mean, about this other character. As you know, Paul had been a real enemy of all the Christians in Jerusalem before his conversion. He was a really devout Jew and believed that Jesus was a charlatan, a sham—a crook, more or less. And anyone who professed faith in Jesus as the Son of God would hide away from Paul—or Saul, as he was called at that time —because they knew that he would have all believers whipped and stoned—sometimes to death.

'Right. Now, after Paul became a Christian he wanted to go and preach about Jesus in Jerusalem, and this chap whose name I mustn't mention went into Jerusalem ahead of Paul to tell the Christians that there was nothing to be scared of now. Paul was coming to teach them about Jesus!

He had been converted to Christ! He would not harm the Christians now! And carrying that message to the Christians in Jerusalem was one of the things that made this man famous—so famous that we still remember him two thousand years later!'

'Is there any place or church named after him?' said Jason.

'Oh, my word, yes! Dozens of churches in this country alone. But, more than that, he is the founder of the Church in Cyprus itself—so all Cypriot Christians look to him as their patron saint.'

'And was he one of the twelve apostles?'

'Funny you should ask that. No, he wasn't—yet he is always described as "The Apostle Bar . . ."'—he stopped himself just in time—I mean, "So-and-So".'

Jason noticed the slip and slotted it away for future reference. 'So, it begins with "Bar",' he thought, and finished his orange Slushpuppy.

Very shortly afterwards he was in his father's study and reaching for *The Bible Encyclopaedia and Concordance*. He looked under 'B' and came to Barabbas. But then he came to Barachel and Barachias and Bariah and Barjesus and Bar-jonah and Barnabas and Barsabas and Bartholomew and Bartimaeus—which one was it?

The Mars Bar seemed an unlikely prospect. Then he thought of looking at his Bible. Matthew, Mark, Luke, John,—The Acts of The Apostles! Sitting on his bed he began to read.

☆ ☆ ☆

Hugo Smart, still sniggering at his success in fooling Cedric, watched him disappear over the brow of the hill on his bike and then he raced back toward Mr Jackson's house.

He rang the doorbell, and the door was opened.

'Mr Jackson—I know the answer! It's—'

The choirmaster held up his hand. 'Sorry, Hugo. Wait till Sunday morning after practice, please. I'll make a note of anyone who calls in the meantime and I'll ask them for the answer in the order in which they came to see me—so you'll be first on the list. OK?'

Just as he said this the phone rang. He picked it up and Hugo heard him say, 'Why, Cedric! You think you know the answer? You're number two on the list, then!'

☆ ☆ ☆

Choir practice on Sunday morning, June 11, came to an end, and excitement was in the air. On the notice board was the final clue, as promised. It ran: 'TODAY IS HIS DAY'.

'Now,' said Mr Jackson, 'the first boy to come to me with an answer was Hugo.'

Hugo glanced nervously at Peter but lounged back comfortably in his chair. 'Easy!' he said. 'It's Dennis.'

There was a silence for just two seconds, then, led by Peter himself, the entire room exploded with laughter. Hugo glowered round at everyone but was careful not to look in either Peter's or Cedric's direction.

The choirmaster said hurriedly, 'No, I don't think there is anyone in the Bible of that name, Hugo. Now, the second boy was Cedric Stevens.'

Cedric had been staring in disbelief at Hugo. 'Hugo, you told me it was Theophilus!' he cried.

'That was because Peter told me it was Dennis!' blurted out Hugo, then realised too late what he had said. Cedric got up from his chair, lifted his heavy hymnbook above his head and was about to bring it down with some force on to Hugo's when Jason intervened and restored order.

'How peculiar,' said Mr Jackson. 'Well, it isn't Theophilus, either. Number three on my list is Jason Webb. Jason?'

'I've found out a bit about him and I read the story in the Acts, and I think it's Barnabas,' said Jason.

'Yes, absolutely right!' The choirmaster led the applause. 'And now, while we're in the mood for clapping,' he said, tossing the Mars Bar to Jason, 'I've got something else to announce. I've been watching the younger boys to see who's been trying hardest lately. One of you is going to be presented with a light blue ribbon by the vicar at this morning's service. Will you all give a big hand to—Cedric Stevens!'

There was another stunned silence while everyone absorbed this astonishing piece of news, but when the applause finally came it was so enthusiastic that it drowned the noise of the church bells ringing for morning service.

And even Jason joined in.

Jason and the Small Baptist

The River Ock is not a noble river. It starts high in the hills to the west of Oakbridge and trickles undecidedly along past the back streets of Oakchester, through woodland and village, and then, with a sudden widening and a brief rush through the sandy soil of Oakhaven, it empties out into the sea.

The bridge which spans the river at Oakbridge gave the village its name, 'Ock' becoming 'oak' through the centuries.

It was a summer Saturday morning and Jason was riding his bike along the lane toward the bridge. A much smaller boy than Jason was sitting on the bridge wall, facing the river, and throwing sticks backwards over his shoulder. Jason was just in time to see a stick flying high in the air across the roadway and disappearing over the opposite side of the bridge to land in the water upstream. The small boy timed it on his watch until it appeared in the water below his dangling feet.

Jason freewheeled quietly up behind him, stopped inches behind his back, and shouted 'Oy!' in his ear—at the same time gripping him firmly round the waist to stop him falling into the river.

There followed a brief struggle and a heated shouting match, but when they had brushed themselves down Jason asked, 'What's the record, then?'

Jason was just in time to see a stick flying high in the air . . .

Cedric Stevens considered exaggerating and saying 'thirty seconds' but decided he would probably be forced to prove it. 'Ten seconds,' he said, defiantly.

'Let's have a go,' said Jason, and sat up on the railing. He took a stick and, looking behind him to judge the angle, whipped it up and back with all the strength in his batting wrist. The seconds flicked past on his watch. Nine, ten, eleven,—twelve! And the stick came bobbing into sight.

'Beat that, then,' said Jason.

'You're bigger'n me!'

'And I'm bigger than both of you,' said a deep voice behind them, and Jason jumped almost as high as Cedric had a few minutes before.

'Mr Davis—hullo!' said Jason. Cedric had disappeared to find more sticks. 'This is a game I invented.' He explained the rules.

'Well, I'm glad I found you, Jason,' said Old Man Davis. 'Now, listen. You know my new granddaughter's being christened at St Matthew's next Sunday. I was wondering if you would be kind enough to do something for me.'

Jason wondered what on earth *he* could do to help with a christening. The two leaned over the railing watching the water while Old Man Davis explained what it was he wanted. Then he reached into his jacket pocket and handed an envelope and a small glass bottle to Jason. 'Take great care of it, won't you. It's nearly 150 years old—last used at my great great grandfather's christening.'

Cedric appeared just as they finished their conversation and picked up the last word. 'Christening?' he said, and dumped an armful of twigs on the grass. 'Is that when they pour water all over a baby?'

'Hardly *all* over,' said the man, and Jason laughed. 'But, yes, that's the general idea. We do it as a sign that we promise to bring the child up to know and love God and his Son Jesus Christ. It can be a baby, an older child—and a grownup, too.'

'What's water got to do with it?' said Cedric, being practical, and Jason was secretly glad the younger boy had asked the question.

The sun was shining and the birds singing on this summer's day, and it was a pleasant enough place to have a lesson. Old Man Davis looked at his watch. 'I can't be long—I've got to get over to Crombie's farm. But very quickly: another word for "Christening" is "Baptism"—'

'Oh, I know *that*,' interrupted Cedric, hurling a stick backwards and nearly getting Old Man Davis in the eye.

'Yes, of course you do,' he said, moving sideways. 'But I wonder if you also knew that it comes from the same word that dyers used—that is, the people who used to dye cloth in different colours. They plunged the cloth under the dyed water, just as John the Baptist took new converts to the Jewish faith and plunged them under the water of the River Jordan and lifted them up again. But what he was doing was giving the new Jewish believer a sign that the old "self" was being buried and the new "self" was coming up out of the grave and being born again—born a second time—fresh, new, starting again with God as his master and guide. Then, later on, when Jesus the Christ began his ministry, John baptized people as Christians—followers of Christ.'

'Well,' said Cedric, hurling another stick backwards with such force that he nearly fell off the railing and baptized himself in the River Ock, 'why don't babies get pushed under the water instead of having it poured over them?'

'Some branches of the Church do just that—not with babies, exactly, but certainly with adults. You've heard of the Baptist Church—there's one in Oakchester. If you go in there you'll find, just in front of the pulpit, a trap door in the floor—a big one, about four or five metres long. If they lifted that up for you, you'd see a sort of small swimming pool. And when someone becomes a Christian, they have a special service in which that person is led down into the water. The minister asks questions about the person's faith, and the new Christian makes promises in front of all the church members—and before God, of course. Then—down into the water and up again!'

'Crumbs!', said Cedric thoughtfully, looking down at the water. Then he said, 'Cor!'

'But, of course, when a baby is baptized—or "christened"—in the Church of England it has the water sprinkled over its head. And it is the parents who are making the promises on their child's behalf. And when the child grows up to be a teenager, he or she will be able to make another, personal confession of faith in Jesus.'

Cedric looked earnestly at Old Man Davis, and said, 'What are those words the vicar always says when he christens a baby—something about father and son?'

'That's the little sentence that makes it clear to everyone standing round that the vicar is baptizing the baby in the name of God—or for God. So he says "I baptize you in the name of the Father, the Son, and the Holy Spirit. Amen".'

Cedric repeated the words after him.

Old Man Davis looked at his watch. 'Gracious me! I must go! G'bye for now!' And he strode off toward Crombie's farm. Jason picked up a stick to try and break his personal best. But Cedric was gazing very thoughtfully into the waters of the River Ock.

☆ ☆ ☆

That afternoon, Jason called to his father who was working in the garden, 'Dad, can I borrow some of your writing paper—and that ruler?'

'You mean "can I *have* some", I suppose,' said his father, leaning on his rake. 'I don't suppose you intend replacing it. Yes, of course you can—but don't take too much. Last time you "borrowed" paper I found Jason Webb cartoons of The Incredible Hulk plastered all round your bedroom and not a single sheet left in my desk. I had to write a letter to my bank manager on a picture postcard of Corfu, I remember.'

Ten minutes later, Jason, head bent low over his work table, was writing. It was not his usual handwriting, but a careful, flowing style. The previous Christmas he had been given a book on calligraphy, and in trying his hand at it he discovered that he could produce very professional-looking script writing. He had done various jobs for the choirmaster by way of notices for the choir notice board, and special headings for the parish magazine.

Now he was working on Old Man Davis's commission: a presentation card to be given to his new granddaughter at her Christening in a week's time. He was enjoying himself; he could hear the football on television downstairs, but even that did not pull him away from his calligraphy. Slowly, the curving black letters flowed from his pen to the white paper.

☆ ☆ ☆

The following Saturday evening, the day before the christening at St Matthew's, Cedric was also absorbed in what he was doing. His birthday had been last week, and his parents had given him a kitten—something he had wanted 'for hundreds of years', as he would tell his friends. Now, he was nursing it in his lap. It was fast asleep. This did not suit Cedric, as he had just made a toy for the kitten in the shape of a ball of silver foil on the end of a long piece of string, and he wanted to see if the kitten liked it.

As he stroked it, he said over and over again, 'In the name of the father, the son and the holy spirit, amen.' Then he looked at his watch and smiled at a secret thought.

☆ ☆ ☆

On that same Saturday evening Jason stood in his bedroom gazing at the now finished lettering on white card. He put his head on one side. Yes, the calligraphy was as good as anything he'd done, and he was pleased with it. It was a poem which Old Man Davis had written himself, and it was dedicated to his granddaughter. Jason read it aloud:

'Lord, bless and keep this little child:
your blessing be her joy,
your keeping, her most certain strength
that nothing can destroy.

'So look upon this little child
and make your face to shine
that she may see, through hopes and fears,
a countenance divine.

'Then may this precious little child
grow in your heavenly grace
which little children long ago
found in Christ's holy face.

'Your peace be with this little child—
not as the world would give;
your peace no mortal understands,
yet in that peace we live.

'We dedicate this little child
in deepest joy and praise;
prepare our hearts to love her well
and lead her in your ways.'

It was bedtime, and he started to get ready for bed. As he put his jacket over the back of a chair there was a small sound of something hard knocking against wood. He looked at his jacket. The sound had come from the region of one of the pockets. He put his hand into the pocket. Something small hard and shiny came between his finger and thumb. Jason caught his breath—it was the bottle! Old Man Davis's bottle! He'd forgotten all about doing the rest of the job!

He threw on his jacket again and bolted downstairs three at a time. Having called out that he would only be a minute he went round to the shed and got his bike out. Pedalling down the lane toward the bridge he thanked his lucky stars that he'd remembered before the baptism tomorrow. What would Old Man Davis have done to him?

At the bridge he propped up his bike against one of the stone piers and went down the grassy bank to the water. He took out the bottle and removed the cork. Then he knelt down and dipped the bottle into the water until the bubbles stopped rising. He took it out, wiped it dry on his handkerchief, corked it and put it in his jacket pocket again.

Unknown to Jason, only a few steps away on the other side of the bridge, Cedric was also kneeling down by the water. Beside him was a Church of England Prayer Book, and in his hands was his new and very small kitten. The Prayer Book was open at the service of The Baptism of Infants.

Cedric cleared his throat and began to read aloud in a high, sing-song voice. The kitten hung between his hands, its front paws outstretched, its hind legs dangling. It miaowed softly. Cedric's voice drifted out into the summer evening, mingling with the buzzing of insects and the gurgling of the river. There came a silence, and then, leaning forward to reach the little inlet of deeper water in front of him, Cedric held the kitten just above the surface. Then, in a louder voice, he sang out:

'I baptize thee in the name of—' and so saying he plunged the kitten into the river until the cold water came up to his elbows.

'Stop! Cedric, Stop!' Jason came pounding down the bank, took hold of Cedric's shoulders and heaved him backwards. Cedric, lying flat on his back and holding the dripping kitten high in the air, stared up at Jason.

'Whatcher do that for!' he said. 'I was baptizing him! Now you've been and gone and spoilt it!' But Jason had thrown his jacket down on the bank, tugged his shirt off and was wrapping the shivering kitten in Marks and Spencer Boys' Wear.

'Listen, you don't baptize kittens, you idiot! They drown if you baptize them. You only baptize *people*. Hey, where's my jacket gone?'

He was just in time to see his jacket floating slowly downstream under the bridge and heading for the sea.

'The bottle! It's in the pocket!' He shoved the bundled-up kitten into Cedric's arms and was about to jump in and run downstream after it when Cedric called out, 'You mean this bottle? It fell out of your pocket just now and started rolling down the bank. I grabbed it.'

The very idea of Cedric being sensible took words out of Jason's mouth. But the sight of his jacket disappearing restored his power of speech and he stuffed the bottle into the pocket of Cedric's trousers.

'Fantastic!' he said. 'Take care of that!' And he waded down stream toward the soggy denim bubble that was his jacket.

☆ ☆ ☆

The baptism service went well. But the highlight was when Old Man Davis stepped up to the font during the service and spoke to the congregation. He told them that the bottle had contained the water for his great great grandfather's christening nearly 150 years before, and that now it had provided the water for his granddaughter—water gathered from the parish's own river.

At the buffet lunch afterwards, Jason's calligraphy and the small bottle stood in a place of honour between the christening cake and the iced buns. Jason and Cedric stood looking alternately at the iced buns and the display.

'If I hadn't grabbed that bottle it would've been in America by now,' said Cedric.

'And if I hadn't found you when I did,' said Jason sternly, 'Your kitten would've been in heaven.'

Cedric sighed. 'Well, at least it would have been baptized,' he said, '—the way John the Baptist did it.' Then he helped himself to his fourth iced bun.

Jason and the Doubting Thomas

Jason was in their garden shed, and it was Saturday. He picked up his bicycle pump, and then put it down again. Then he balanced a tin of screws on an oil can and a jar full of paint thinners on top of that. Then he dismantled the construction and chewed his thumb. He touched a spider in the middle of its web and frightened the life out of it.

Jason, too, was scared stiff. But not of the spider.

Yesterday he had been called by the Head to see Mr Craig, the new P.E. teacher, whose claim to fame was that he had once been a high-wire and trapeze artist with a circus troupe.

'Sit down, Webb,' said the Head. 'Mr Craig, as you know, will be balancing and walking on the high wire for the school fête next Saturday. One of the things he will do is—well, you explain,' he said to the P.E. teacher.

Mr Craig leaned against the windowsill looking at Jason. 'What I need is a partner,' he said. 'One of my acts involves taking someone—not too big—up on to the wire with me. For the entertainment of the crowd I pretend to make a random choice from among the people watching.'

Jason was twisting his quiff of hair and swallowing hard. He thought he knew what was coming.

'Now, I've watched you at P.E. and I think you would be exactly right for the job. Would you like to do it? You'd be absolutely safe. What's more, I'm being sponsored by parents, and all the money we raise is going to a very good charity.'

Jason gulped. 'Le-VITicus! On the high wire—me? What, balancing?'

'No, no. What happens is this.' And the next five minutes was spent in telling Jason what he would be asked to do, thirty feet up in the air.

At the end, he had agreed to do it. But his dreams were very scary ones for the nights that followed.

☆ ☆ ☆

The day came nearer. At choir practice on Friday, a week and a day before the fête, the choir prepared for St Thomas's day, July 3. The choirmaster spent a few minutes with the boys to explain who St Thomas was. Jason was too busy imagining himself up on the high wire, higher than the main school buildings, to take in much of what was being said. But he woke up when he heard Mr Jackson say, 'And that's something you could all copy yourselves—Thomas's habit of making absolutely sure.'

For some reason, the phrase stuck in Jason's mind for the rest of the evening and kept popping up at intervals through Saturday. He was cleaning his bike on the front path when Old Man Davis walked by.

'Afternoon, Jason! Put some beef into it!'

'Hullo, Mr Davis.' They chatted for a minute, then Jason blurted out, 'Mr Davis, d'you know why Thomas—Jesus's disciple, that is—why he had the habit of making absolutely sure?'

'Ah! What a very good question! I imagined you've heard about Thomas at choir practice!' At Jason's nod he went on, 'Well, Jesus had just been put on the cross by the Roman soldiers at the demand of the Jews. He had died, and been dead for three days. Then, people started reporting that they had seen Jesus alive! Well, his disciple, Thomas, heard the stories, but he had this habit of always making absolutely sure of something before he believed it. So he said to them, "Until I've actually seen the marks in his hands where they nailed him to the cross, and put my finger in the wound that the Roman sword made in his side, I'm not going to believe he's alive". And you can understand why, can't you! After all, if he believed Jesus was alive he would have to believe that Jesus really was the Son of God. And that would change his whole life. He would be committed! There would be no escape!'

Jason sat on the saddle and tried to balance without his feet on the ground as he said, 'What happened to him after that?'

'Oh, he went on to travel way out east to Asia, and he set up one of the earliest churches. That was in India. If you went to South India today you'd find that the Christians there are called the Mar Thoma Church.'

They said goodbye and Jason watched his friend walk on down the lane. He stayed like that for some time, a rag in his hand. Then he started rubbing the handlebars with a new vigour. He had made up his mind. He knew what he would do.

☆ ☆ ☆

'Hullo, Jason! Come in,' said the P.E. teacher. Jason wiped his feet on the front door mat of the teacher's house and went into the hallway. 'Want some Coke? A piece of fruit cake?'

Jason sat on the edge of Mr Craig's best armchair with a can of Coke in one hand and a slice of fruit cake in the other.

He was nervous. What he had to ask was a favour. But it was a favour that would make him feel a whole lot better about the fête next week. He took a deep breath.

'It's about next Saturday, sir. Would you do something for me?' he said.

☆ ☆ ☆

Jason woke up with bright sunshine flickering through his bedroom curtains that moved in a morning breeze. He lay blinking at his Space Station wallpaper, then at the curtains. Jolly good, he thought—it's Saturday. Then the awful truth hit him. Today he had to go on the high wire. A tight feeling crept through his stomach, and he swallowed.

He couldn't lie there, thinking. He swung his legs out of bed, and made for the bathroom. 'It's higher than the school roof,' he thought as he washed his face. And, brushing his teeth, 'It's going to take a whole minute to cross!' Pulling on his jeans he thought, 'Supposing the wire breaks?' And finally, running downstairs to breakfast, he thought, 'I'm not going to do it!'

His mother rumpled his hair—her usual 'good-morning' greeting—and his carefully plastered-down quiff sprang at once to attention. 'Oh, by the way, Cedric's father dropped an envelope in before you were awake. It's a note from Cedric, apparently.'

Jason groaned a bubbling sort of groan as he was in the middle of drinking his tea. He tore open the envelope. There were three words on the piece of paper:

SURPRISE, SURPRISE!!!!!! CEDRIC.

He arrived at the school playing field an hour before necessary. Hectic activities were under way, with tents being erected, flags hoisted on to brailings, balloons being inflated and trestle tables being carried from the school hall. The fire brigade were there, with Mr Craig directing operations as, from thirty feet up on the fire-engine's extending ladder, they lifted the metal struts into position.

Jason's watch chimed the hour. Ten o'clock. One hour to go. The minutes crawled by.

☆ ☆ ☆

'Ladies and Gentlemen!' called the Head over the loudspeaker system. 'In five minutes' time you will see the amazing, exciting, unbelievable escapade of our very own P.E. teacher, Trevor Craig! He is going to climb up the very shaky-looking rope ladder that leads up to the high wire, and he is going to defy gravity by walking along the wire and back again! Don't miss this remarkable feat of bravery! Trevor Craig has been sponsored by you all, and the funds he has raised will go to the excellent charity selected by the school governors. Gather round now, ladies and gentlemen, and get a good view of this exciting event!'

Jason stood smiling happily up at the high wire that swung slightly in the breeze. All but the smallest twinge of fear had left him. Now, he was content. He was actually looking forward to his adventure.

The P.E. teacher came up to him, dressed in green overalls and with goggles pushed up on his forehead. 'Ready?' he whispered. 'Don't forget to look surprised when I pick you!' He went to the microphone and all the chatter and laughter stopped. The crowd left the stalls and pressed round him. They listened as he told them what he was going to do. They watched him move through the crowd as he looked for someone to go up on the high wire with him. Who would be brave enough, they were asking each other. They watched as he came to Jason. They tried to hear the conversation.

They had gone about two metres when it happened . . .

Then, as the two walked up to the microphone together there was a burst of applause. The applause continued after the announcement of Jason's name and followed the man and boy to the foot of the thin rope ladder.

Trevor Craig strapped a webbing harness round Jason's waist and up between his legs, forming a seat. Then he stood behind him, lifted him up and hooked him to the straps on his own chest by two large shiny clasps. A long steel bolt was pushed through the clasps, and all was ready.

'OK?'

'OK!', said Jason. But at that moment the head walked up to them, carrying a microphone. And beside him was Cedric Stevens.

'And now, ladies and gentlemen,' he said, 'One more detail! Cedric Stevens here,' he patted the head of the small boy beside him, 'has agreed to let Gerald, his pet gerbil, walk the wire as well! Jason is going to hold Cedric's gerbil all the way across and back again! And no less than 150 pupils have sponsored Cedric's gerbil to do so!'

Jason gulped. 'WHAT?' he almost shouted at Cedric. 'You never said anything about this!'

'Yes I did,' smiled Cedric, ever so sweetly. 'Sort of, anyway. In my note! Remember—"surprise, surprise"? Thanks ever so much!' And he put the gerbil into Jason's unwilling hands and sauntered off.

Speechless, Jason glared at his retreating back. He cupped his hands round the small, warm, furry shape, and concentrated on their ascent of the flexible ladder. Step by step, the ground slipped further and further away. The safety net looked more like a spider's web below them.

They reached the top, and Jason held his breath as Mr Craig put one foot on the taut, quivering wire.

'OK, Jason? Just relax and enjoy it!' said the voice just behind and above his head, and with that he felt himself carried forward. Slowly, smoothly, they went out on to the wire.

They had gone about two metres when it happened. The gerbil, feeling that life was not all it should be inside Jason's increasingly hot hands, made a bid for freedom. Gathering all its strength, it leaped. It shot out of Jason's grasp and on to his shoulder. Jason made a wild grab at it, and wobbled violently in his webbing seat. The movement upset Mr Craig's balance and for a horrible few seconds the long balancing pole he carried swung up and down as he tried to keep his balance. They swayed from side to side. A gasp went up from the watching crowd below. Slowly, the swaying stopped, the pole was horizontal again, and they moved gently forward.

'Jason,' said the P.E. teacher quietly in his ear, 'just leave the gerbil alone. Just leave him, whatever he does.'

What the gerbil did was plenty. It sniffed Jason's ear. It got into his hair and scratched his head for him. It peered down inside his shirt collar, and, deciding that it looked interesting down there, dived into the gloomy depths. Once there, it chased its tail, investigated small pimples and tried to scale the heights of Jason's stomach, chest and throat. Jason kept his nerve and spent the time deciding what he was going to do to Cedric.

The return journey along the wire went without further incident. Trevor Craig's hand reached out for the top of the support mast and together they swung round on to the ladder and slithered down to the grass below.

Jason, with the gerbil now firmly in his hands again, was carried shoulder-high by the cheering crowd to the refreshment tent.

☆ ☆ ☆

The next day, before Sunday morning choir practice, the choirmaster said to Jason, 'Oh, by the way, the head let me in on your little secret—in other words, I knew that you knew *you* were going to be picked for the high-wire stunt. But something puzzles me. I was watching you yesterday when you arrived very early at the field, and you were plainly extremely nervous. Then, just before you did the act itself, you were as happy and calm as anything. Why?'

'I took your advice and copied Thomas, sir.'

'Copied Thomas? How?'

'Thomas's habit of making absolutely sure,' said Jason, 'just as you told us last week. I went to Mr Craig's house and said I'd be less nervous about trusting him if I could see him actually go up on the wire first. And he did—nobody noticed except me. And then I was sure he could do it.'

The choirmaster smiled. 'I'm glad you were listening to that bit, at least,' he said. 'But there's something else you should remember. After Thomas had seen the evidence of Jesus's wounds, Jesus reminded him that God much prefers us to believe *without* asking for proof. Oh, by the way, have you tried writing down the words "THOMAS'S HABIT OF MAKING ABSOLUTELY SURE"? I think you'd find something very interesting about the initial letters.'

Jason told him he would, as soon as he got home after church. But first, he said, he had to have a little chat with Cedric.

Jason and the Harvest Solo

It was September, the time of year when grownups started moaning about the days getting shorter and farmers, like Jason's father, moaned about the weather.

One Friday evening, as usual, Jason got on his bike and started off for choir practice. The church was only half a mile along the lane; the first half was hard work, all uphill. He stood on the pedals and pumped his way up round the sharp bend by the Davis's farm gate, up past the Crombie's big farm on the left, up the long climb through the tunnel formed by the oak trees and past the old, black, silent derelict barn that always made him pedal just that little bit faster.

Then it was downhill all the way to St Matthew's. The wind rushed in his face and even flattened the famous tuft of hair. He crouched low over the handlebars as he whistled past the churchyard and imagined he was doing over a hundred-and-forty down the straight at Brands Hatch. He skidded a long, noisy and delicious skid through the dust of St Matthew's entrance yard, locked his bike on to the rack by the side door and, with half a dozen others who had just arrived, ran through the corridor to the choir vestry.

It was a quite ordinary choir practice. An anthem to be learned, the basses, tenors and altos to be taken through their parts, hymns to be brushed up, and Cedric to be told off for trying to balance his hymn book on his head, kicking the boy next to him and, with his heavily-loaded folder, swatting a fly which had landed on the head of the boy in front.

But halfway through the practice the choirmaster reminded them that it was the Harvest service in two weeks' time, and that he had an important announcement to make. He had been asked by the vicar to suggest some way in which one particular verse of a hymn might be emphasised, and he had now decided that one of the boys should sing it as a solo. Between tonight and the next practice he was going to choose someone to sing it. It was No 291, and now they would all sing it right through.

Everybody sang as he had never sung before. Every eye watched every movement of the choirmaster's hands as he conducted; every head was up, every mouth open, every voice gave every note precisely the right value. Each boy made his crescendos swell beautifully from *piano* to *forte* and each *diminuendo* fall smoothly from full-throated sound to little more than a whisper. Every word was clear. Every boy wanted to be the chosen soloist.

There was one line in the hymn that particularly attracted Jason. It contained a word that was at once puzzling and beautiful.

At last, the hymn and the practice came to an end. Outside in the yard, Jason, having had a very satisfactory but not too serious fight with his two friends Spud and John, got on his bike and pedalled happily up the hill.

☆ ☆ ☆

The following week, choir practice had a certain air of excitement about it. Each singer sang as well as—if not better than—he had the previous week. Cedric had to be told off only twice. Ten minutes before the end, Mr Jackson said, 'Now, we're going to sing the special harvest hymn and I'm going to point to each one of you in turn to sing one line by yourself'.

The hymn began, with everyone singing. The choir-master's finger pointed at a boy in the front row for line two, and his slightly quavering voice sang it, a little stronger at the end than at the beginning. Everyone sang for another line, then the finger pointed again and another, steadier, voice sang.

Jason's heart thumped. When would his turn come? His voice sounded croaky in his own ears—he would be terrible! The thought had barely entered his head when Mr Jackson's finger caught him at long range straight between the eyes. The page blurred in front of him; in panic fear he had lost the place. Then, with a split second to spare, he found it.

That single line of a hymn lasted longer than he had ever imagined it could. Every note was a hurdle to jump, every word a pothole to fall into.

Mr Jackson stood by the piano. 'By next week,' he said, 'I'll have decided who is to sing the solo verse. Sing it over to yourselves in the bath, get to know it really well.' After the prayer everyone went home a little less boisterously than usual. Everyone had something on his mind. Jason had something particular on his. Puzzling, yet beautiful.

☆ ☆ ☆

The next day was Saturday. Jason finished his breakfast and was just going out to the shed to start work on retouching some scratches on his newly-painted skateboard when his mother asked him to go to the village shops. Armed with shopping list and money, he set off up the hill.

He was passing the gate to the Davis's farm when he saw Old Man Davis coming down the drive on the farm tractor. What happened then was one of those odd moments when your brain works at double speed and does two things at once. Jason's brain told him to open the gate for the tractor and to ask Mr Davis a question.

He lifted the heavy iron bar from its socket and heaved against the heavy white gate.

'Why, thanks very much, Jason!'

'That's all right. Er—Mr Davis, can you spare a minute?' The bang-bang-bang of the tractor engine slowed and stopped. 'Anything for you, Jason,' smiled the old man. 'What d'you want?'

'Well, I know you go round to chapels all over the place, preaching and so on, and you know about—well, God, and Church, and religion and that, and I've got a question.'

Old Man Davis patted the folded sack beside his seat on the tractor, and laughed. 'Come on up here! You know there's nothing I like more than talking!' Jason swung himself up on to the high metal step and sat down. Mr Davis was one of those people you could feel, well, at ease with.

'We were singing a hymn at choir practice,' he began. 'It's all about Harvest and that, and God giving us daily bread, and cornfields and stuff. But there's a bit I can't understand —but it sounds good. It's about "firstfruits", and I want to know what firstfruits are.'

Old Man Davis looked down at the boy beside him. What wonderful questions Jason did ask! Boys of his age didn't normally ask questions about ancient Hebrew festivals. But what a question! What a beautiful question! He could talk for an hour about it. How was he going to answer this one in a couple of minutes? He cleared his throat.

'If you'd been a farmer's son several thousand years ago and you happened to have been born out in the Middle

East—let's say in Jerusalem—to a Hebrew family, round about May-June time every year the whole family would start the great business of preparing the "firstfruits". In other words, just one bunch of the very first wheat to be harvested that year, a bag of the very first grapes to be picked in the vineyard, the first lamb to be born that year. And not only that; if a new baby had been born in the family that year, the baby was treated as one of the firstfruits.

'Then the whole family would go up to the great Temple and they would go in and offer their gifts—the whole year's "firstfruits"—to God. It was a way of saying that they knew everything came from God, and a way of saying "Thank you" to him.'

'I hope they brought the baby back home again!' said Jason, and immediately wished he hadn't.

'Most certainly they did,' answered Old Man Davis solemnly.

'Well, I've got to get the shopping. But, one thing: we're not ancient Hebrews and this isn't the Middle East. So why do we have Harvest at Church? And in any case, we can't all bring firstfruits. Some of us bring tins of pineapple and packets of biscuits!'

'Yes. Well, very quickly: our church in the village—St Matthew's—is part of a tremendous group of people all over the world called Christians. They are named after Jesus, whose title was "The Christ", who was a Hebrew and lived two thousand years ago. He was born, in a miraculous way, up in Bethlehem. He turned out to be God himself, in the form of an ordinary man. People turned to him, listened to what he had to say. They were amazed to have God in front of them, talking to them. Many people began to follow him, metaphorically—you know what "metaphorically" means? Yes, of course!—metaphorically as well as actually.

They started to live according to his teaching—which was only how they should have been living, anyway, all the time. In two thousand years they have grown to be this tremendous company of people called "The Church". And, naturally, because the Church began among Hebrew people, we have kept a lot of their festivals, and Harvest is one of them. I've missed out a lot—but I hope that helps?'

In the shop, Jason was so busy thinking about Hebrew firstfruits that he forgot to get the potatoes.

☆ ☆ ☆

It was at choir practice the following week that Mr Jackson announced the name of the soloist.

Cedric Stevens.

The whole choir was aghast. Cedric, the clown! Cedric, the trouble-maker! The injustice of it erupted.

'Leviticus!' exclaimed Jason, 'he was the last one to join the choir, sir!'

'He's a freak!' said another.

'QUIET!' said the choirmaster. 'I have chosen Cedric because I believe he has exactly the right kind of voice for this particular occasion. I have made it quite clear to him that his is not the best voice in the choir—yet, and certainly not the strongest or the most accurate. But it has a quality which I have decided is exactly right for this occasion. And there is one other consideration which has finally made up my mind—but I am keeping that to myself.'

Jason boiled inside. He was angry, not only with Cedric and Mr Jackson, but with himself for having this wretched feeling that he was about to cry. Him! Cry! He blew his nose as hard as he could and stretched his eyes as far open as they would go. That helped.

☆ ☆ ☆

Sunday morning came; the church was stacked to the windowsills with wheatsheaves and grapes and apples and potatoes. There were enormous loaves of bread made to look like bundles of corn, fantastic arrays of flowers round the lectern and pulpit; the choirstalls had fruit and vegetables lining the front of Decani and Cantoris. The air in the church was heavy with the scent of autumn. A yellow morning sun shone through the south and east windows and turned white surplices to pale gold.

The second reading was over, and the vicar was standing in his stall. Jason looked across to Cedric, pink-faced, on Cantoris.

'We now sing the hymn number 291,' said the vicar. 'Verse two will be sung as a solo by a member of the choir, and I ask you to follow the words in your books. Hymn 291.'

The hymn went very well:

'To you, O Lord, our hearts we raise
in hymns of adoration:
accept our sacrifice of praise,
our shouts of exultation . . .'

Cedric's solo verse was a little on the quiet side, Jason thought, but the effect was electric:

'And now on this our festal day
your love to us expressing,
our gifts before you, Lord, we lay,
the firstfruits of your blessing . . .'

. . . the effect was electric.

The church, packed with people, was so still it could have been empty. And yet, as that small voice sang, the building was filled to overflowing with an atmosphere quite different from anything he had experienced before. A fleeting image of the Temple in Jerusalem flashed across his mind, of the firstfruits being brought in, the grapes, the lamb, the tiny squawking new member of the family.

After the service, when the last boy had rushed out of the choir vestry door, Jason went up to the choirmaster.

'Sir,' he said, going bright red and wishing he'd gone straight home instead. 'You know about firstfruits, and everything, don't you. Well, I thought just now that with Cedric singing the solo, and him being the newest member of the choir, it was a bit like the choir offering a—well, a—'

'Firstfruit?' smiled Mr Jackson. 'As a matter of fact, that's exactly what I had in mind,' he said.

From the top of the hill, Jason's bike flew like the wind.

Jason and the Musical Saint

'Where's Cecilia?' called Jason from the top of the stairs. 'She's pinched my library book again! Sisters!'

His mother called back from the kitchen, 'She's down here helping me wash up. She says she hasn't taken it and have you looked under your pillow where you probably hid it last night when you should have been asleep?'

He groaned. It *was* under his pillow, and he wondered how she had known. She must have seen the light of his torch under the door and made a blind guess. 'Sisters!' he muttered. Then he kicked off his shoes, switched on his bedside light, flopped on to his bright blue duvet and began to read.

His father was re-decorating the bathroom, and the smell of paint being burnt off the door and the roar of the blowlamp did nothing for his enjoyment of the book. But it was a good story and he was soon lost in it. It was about a boy who wanted to become a journalist—Jason's own ambition. A real reporter had arrived at the boy's house enquiring about a gold bullion robbery. The boy had asked if he could go back with the reporter and have a look round the newspaper office. They were in the reporter's car now and found they were being chased up the motorway by a gang in a minibus. At that moment Jason heard the phone ring downstairs.

Mrs Webb called out, 'Jason, it's for you—Cedric Stevens wants you. Sounds as if he's got a cold.'

'Oh, no!' growled Jason, slapping the open book over his face. 'Anyone but Cedric!'

☆ ☆ ☆

When Jason arrived at the Stevens' house Cedric was charming in a snuffling sort of way . . . 'Gosh—thaks ever so buch for cubbig rou'd!'

''S'all right,' said Jason, ungraciously and with some suspicion. 'What's the problem?'

'Well, as I said, Mum and Dad gave me this camera for my birthday and none of us can see how to . . .' and he fumbled with the instruction book and handed Jason the camera. Jason had a similar camera himself, and he quickly worked it out. Then he asked for the film and demonstrated the loading process. He told him how to keep the lens free from finger smudges which make pale, fuzzy pictures. 'And for a close-up of just one person you hold it like—' he handed Cedric the camera and put the small boy's hands in the right position for taking a picture '—like that. Point it at me. That's right. Now, when you want to take a close-up of two people side by side, like this' he said, reaching for Cedric's teddy bear on the settee and putting it up beside his own face, 'you turn the camera flat so that it makes a wide picture—that's it—Bless you!' he added, as Cedric sneezed.

Jason was there for another half-hour, pointing out all the important bits in the instruction book. By the time he waved goodbye to the family at their front door and began cycling home, he found that, much to his surprise, he'd rather enjoyed himself.

He free-wheeled to the garden shed and was surprised to find the door standing wide open. He put his bike inside, shut the door and let himself in through the house front door. A banging noise came from upstairs. People were

'Leviticus! What on earth—'

shouting. His mother was calling, 'It's all right, Cecilia, Daddy's almost through—stand clear, darling! Keep right back!'

Jason leaped up the stairs. 'Leviticus! What on earth—?' He could hardly believe his eyes. His father was making a wild swing at the bathroom door with the big axe that lived in the garden shed. Already badly damaged, the bottom panel now splintered into a jagged hole, and his father put his head through into the bathroom. 'Come on, darling, carefully, now! Through here . . . that's it!'

Cecilia, her face wet with the steam that poured out of the gaping hole in the door and bright red with the heat, crawled out on to the landing. She stood up shakily and started to cry as Mrs Webb comforted her. Then, gracefully, her crimson face subsiding into her snow-white bathrobe, she slithered to the floor in a dead faint.

☆ ☆ ☆

When Jason arrived at choir practice the following evening his story soon drew a crowd. Mr Jackson stood by the piano, listening. 'And there was my dad bashing the bathroom door down!' Jason was saying. 'Apparently, my sister had gone in for a bath, then the door stuck when she tried to come out. Dad had been burning all the paint off the door and the steam had swelled the wood and jammed it. So he gets our enormous axe'—Jason indicated something about two metres long with a head the size of a dustbin lid—'and bashes it down in one go. One-handed, I think,' he added, casually.

The choirmaster had joined the group. 'Did you say she fainted? From the steam and heat?'

'Yes, sir—why?' said Jason.

'And this was Cecilia, your sister?'

'Yes.'

'In the bathroom?'

'Yes.' Jason looked puzzled. 'Why, sir?'

Mr Jackson rubbed his hands together and grinned. 'You'll see,' he said. 'You'll see!' He went to the piano and was about to sit down when he said, 'I hope she's recovered?' Jason nodded, still puzzled, and practice began.

It ended five minutes earlier than usual. Mr Jackson stood leaning against the piano. 'Now I'm going to tell you why I seemed a bit excited about Cecilia's unfortunate experience.

'Very shortly after the time of Christ there was a young girl called Cecilia living in the city of Rome. She was a Christian, and she was engaged to be married. The boy she was going to marry, however, was not a Christian—he was a pagan. Now, this was difficult. Christians and pagans just did not marry each other. The girl had long talks with the boy and eventually he decided to be baptized into the Christian faith. Soon afterwards, so did his brother.

'But times were bad for Christians in Rome, and one day both the boy and his brother were put to death. Cecilia, now a widow, was also threatened. She was brought before the Prefect and told to bow down to a Roman god. She flatly refused, and the soldiers were ordered to take her away and kill her. Now,' said the choirmaster, 'can anyone guess how she was to be put to death?'

'Suffocate her in her bathroom!' called a boy from the back row, and everyone laughed. Jason glared at him.

'That's right,' said Mr Jackson. Jason swung round to face the choirmaster again.

'Yes, they shoved her into her private bathroom, turned on all the steam—it was a kind of Turkish bath—and then locked her in. So now you can see why I was so amazed at Jason's story. This young girl was none other than Saint Cecilia—the Patron Saint of Musicians. Her "Saint's Day" is this week, November 22nd. And why this connection with music? We think it is because the very first thing ever written about her, in AD 545, described her as "singing to God in her heart" while the musicians played at her wedding. She is often shown in stained glass windows as an organist.'

'My sister can play the organ, too,' said Jason. And as he said it a look came into his eyes that anyone who knew him would recognise. It was the look which meant that he had just had a fantastic idea. But Mr Jackson was speaking again.

'Well, the sad end of the story is that she did die—but they failed to kill her by suffocation and beheaded her instead. The executioner struck three unsuccessful blows, and finally he left her, still alive. She lay dying for three days. Some years later her house was turned into a place where the local Christians—the Church, as we call a group of Christians—could meet for worship each Sunday.'

When they were dismissed, Jason was first out.

☆ ☆ ☆

'*Oakchester Gazette*,' said a voice at the other end of the phone.

'Hullo—this is Jason Webb speaking, from Oakbridge. I've got a news story I think you'd like to print.'

'Hang on, I'll give you the News Desk.' Jason could hardly keep still for excitement. At last, he had a real news story. He was on the way to being a real reporter.

'News Desk?' said a voice in his ear.

☆ ☆ ☆

'I just hope,' said Mrs Webb to Jason as the *Gazette* photographer squeezed past her to get yet another angle on Cecilia crawling through the broken bathroom door, 'I just hope that it's all going to be worth it. It's all very well, you phoning the paper, but I've got work to do!'

The girl from the *Gazette* patted her shoulder. 'Mrs Webb,' she said, 'you should be proud of Jason. He's given us a wonderful story—and we can tie it in beautifully with the St Matthew's Church Roof Fund Appeal. It's going to be a full page, and it comes out on the day before St Cecilia's Day! Now, the photographer wants a picture of him pointing to the axe. After that, can I have a few words with him while the photographer takes Cecilia down to the church for pictures of her at the organ—like the Saint?'

And so the wheels of the local newspaper industry slowly turned, ignoring Mrs Webb's complaints, drawing out of Jason all kinds of family history he never thought he knew, extracting from the vicar the story of Saint Cecilia and her martyrdom, and emptying the choirmaster of all the titbits of musical information connected with the saint.

Time passed slowly for Jason after the reporter and photographer had left the Webb household. His mind was seldom on school work. He was in a constant daydream about the coming Saturday morning when the *Gazette* would blazon his story—his own story!—across its pages. Would it be a double-page spread? With a very big headline? Would his name be in heavy type?

Cedric hardly featured at all in his thoughts. When they caught sight of each other at school or in the street Jason noticed nothing strange about him. When Cedric was standing in the playground with a group of boys round him on Thursday, laughing at some joke or other, Jason hardly saw him. When Cedric quickly pocketed something small as Jason came round the corner of the school entrance on the Friday afternoon, with six giggling small boys scattering as he approached, the ace reporter saw nothing.

☆ ☆ ☆

Saturday morning was dark. Jason sat up in bed, switched on his bedside lamp and squinted at his watch. The reason for the lack of daylight became clear. It was only half-past four. He lay back, hands behind his head. The newspaper shop in the High Street opened at six o'clock. The papers were delivered by van shortly before and dumped outside the door. Jason pondered. If he got up at five o'clock and dressed slowly, he could creep into the shed and get his bike and go along towards Oakchester. He'd see the news van coming, turn round and follow it back to the village shop. He could probably slip one copy of the *Gazette* out of the bundle before the shop opened.

Cedric, unknown to Jason, also woke up at half-past four. He, too, wondered if he should get up extra quietly and slip along to the shop, only six doors away along the High Street, to get the first copy of the *Gazette*. But he dozed off while he was thinking about it and woke with a start to find it was nearly half-past five.

And so it was that Jason and Cedric, approaching from opposite directions, arrived at the shop at the same moment. After a brief exchange of surprise at seeing each other they found that they both wanted to see the *Gazette* as quickly as possible. Two bundles of newspapers lay there.

Jason eased one copy out from between the string binding and gave it to Cedric. He decided it was his good deed for the day. Then he eased another copy out, sat on the doorstep and scanned the front page.

There was nothing about Cecilia. There was nothing on pages two, three, four or five. He opened page six. There, across pages six and seven, ran the headline: 'Oakbridge Saint's Namesake Suffers Martyr's Agony'. Below, with the sub-heading 'Father Smashes Bathroom Door with Axe' was the picture of Cecilia crawling out of the gaping hole.

Jason was just reading the caption to the picture when Cedric, sprawled on his stomach across the pavement reading the same double-page spread, howled with laughter. Jason scowled at him and looked back again at the page. Then he saw it.

Boxed round with a fancy rule was a photograph of himself. Not the picture of him standing pointing at the axe, but a slightly fuzzy photo of him, his pointed tuft of hair sticking up even more than usual, holding Cedric's teddy bear against his cheek. Underneath was the caption:

> *'Cecilia Webb's brother Jason, who reported the story to us, cuddles his favourite teddy bear at his Oakbridge home. Picture by Cedric Stevens.'*

Jason's jaw dropped. Then he threw down the paper and scrambled to his feet. But Cedric, his shrill laughter and explosive sneezes echoing down the empty street, was already halfway to his own front door.

He was running very, very fast indeed.